PHA

MARINA TSVETAEVA was born in Mc
became famous as the founder of wł
Arts and a pianist mother who war
herself had renounced. 'Born not ir
poetry from childhood on, and at th
poems at her own expense. At nineteen sne maiiivu ov.g-,
from a family associated with the 19th-century revolutionary organisation 'The
People's Will'. She gave birth to two daughters, in 1912 and 1917. In the Civil War
which followed the 1917 Revolution, Sergey joined the White Army, fighting the
Bolsheviks, and was away with the army when Marina, poverty-stricken and
unable to hold down a job, placed her children temporarily in an orphanage,
where the younger one died of starvation.

In May 1922 she left Russia with her surviving daughter, Alya. After a few
months in Berlin, she moved to a suburb of Prague, rejoining her husband.
Here she wrote most of her 'lyrical satire' *The Ratcatcher*, and her son Georgy
was born. In 1925 she moved with her family to a suburb of Paris. In Paris she
published poetry and prose in the Russian émigré journals, as well as two plays,
Ariadne (1927) and *Phaedra* (1928). Struggling with daily life and constantly
writing, Tsvetaeva remained in France until her fatal return to Russia in 1939
to join her husband and daughter, who had returned before her. Sergey had
become a Soviet sympathiser and without her knowledge had begun, while in
France, to work for the Soviet secret police.

In Soviet Russia it was still a time of persecutions, arrests and fear. Marina
was confronted by harsh living conditions and by grief after grief. Her sister
had been arrested and sent to a prison camp; soon after Marina's arrival, her
daughter Alya was arrested and also sent to a camp; shortly after that, her
husband too was arrested, to be executed two years later. She had few friends
and little income; the political atmosphere was oppressive. In August 1941, after
Russia entered the war, she was evacuated with her son to a distant small town,
Yelábuga. Ten days after arriving there, she hanged herself. Her body was buried
in a common grave. Not long afterwards, her son enlisted in the Soviet army; he
was killed in action at the age of nineteen.

Tsvetaeva's oeuvre consists of twelve volumes of lyric poems, fourteen long
poems, eight plays and about fifty essays, many of them autobiographical.

ANGELA LIVINGSTONE is Professor Emeritus, University of Essex, where she
taught literature (mainly Russian) for thirty-one years. Among her publications
are *Lou Andreas-Salomé* (her life and writings), 1984, four books on Pasternak
(most recently *The Marsh of Gold: Pasternak's Writings on Inspiration and
Creation*, 2008), and two books presenting her translations of work by Tsvetaeva
with commentary: *Art in the Light of Conscience: Eight Essays on Poetry*, 1992,
reissued 2010, and *The Ratcatcher: A Lyrical Satire*, 1999.

Also translated and introduced by Angela Livingstone
in Angel Classics:

The Ratcatcher: A lyrical satire by Marina Tsvetaeva

MARINA TSVETAEVA
PHAEDRA

A drama in verse

with New Year's Letter *and other long poems*

Translated with an introduction and notes by
ANGELA LIVINGSTONE

ANGEL BOOKS
London

First published in Great Britain in 2012 by
Angel Books, 3 Kelross Road, London N5 2QS

www.angelclassics.com

Translation, introduction and notes
copyright © Angela Livingstone 2012

A CIP catalogue record for this book is available from the British
Library

ISBN 978-0-946162-81-9

This book is printed on acid free paper conforming to the British
Library recommendations and to the full American standard

Typeset in 10 on 12½ pt Minion Pro by
Ray Perry, Norfolk
Printed and bound in the UK by the MPG Books Group,
Bodmin and King's Lynn

Contents

Acknowledgements

Several people have assisted me with this book. Above all, I wish to thank my publisher and editor Antony Wood for his innumerable excellent suggestions for the translation of *Phaedra* and his extremely helpful comments on all the book's components. Mikhail Gasparov (alas, now deceased) once sent me indispensable notes on my translation of 'Poem of the Air'; Yuliya Brodovskaya helped greatly with 'New Year's Letter'. My renderings of 'Attempt at a Room' and of parts of *Phaedra* were enhanced by suggestions from Gerry Smith. For vital help with Tsvetaeva's more difficult vocabulary I am indebted to Anna Chernova, Natalia Gogolitsyna and Masha Karp. Discussions with Lazar Fleishman and with Konstantin Polivanov have been valuable. For detailed responses to my English translations and commentaries, I am grateful to Lindajo Bartholomew, Susan Biver and Kay Stevenson. And endlessly grateful to my son Ben Livingstone for his encouragement and patient help with the computer.

For the original impulse to attempt a translation of *Phaedra*, I remain grateful to C.K. Williams and his enthusiasm for Tsvetaeva's work.

Fifty or so lines from the Servant's speech at the beginning of scene three of *Phaedra*, from 'I've had my fill . . .' to '. . . beside your father', were published in a slightly different version in *Cardinal Points*, No. 12, vol. 1, edited by Irina Mashinski and Robert Chandler, Stosvet Publishing House, New York, 2010, pages 160–61; and shorter excerpts from 'New Year's Letter', 'Poem of the Air' and 'Attempt at a Room' were also published in the same issue of *Cardinal Points*, pages 157, 158 and 159–60. Earlier versions of 'Poem of the Air' and 'New Year's Letter' appeared in *Modern Poetry in Translation*, nos 21 and 22, 2003 respectively, edited by Daniel Weissbort.

A.L.

Introduction

Я камень и пламень (I am stone and flame)
Letter to Boris Pasternak, April 1926[1]

TSVETAEVA is one of the great Russian poets of the twentieth century.
She is also one of the most solitary. As Joseph Brodsky said, 'Tsvetaeva
stands all alone in Russian literature, very, very much off by herself'.[2]
Many have sought to say what it is in her work that is incomparable.
One commentator finds her style 'classical, terse, quick, elliptical: *on
a tightrope*';[3] another sees in it 'all feelings strained, bared to the root';[4]
a third – 'the charm of a lavish generosity, openness, readiness to take
everything to its furthest limit';[5] a fourth sums up her spirit as 'incandes-
cent'.[6] All note tension and energy, 'existence on the edge',[7] an unusually
impassioned intelligence. In talking of her verse drama *Phaedra*, in
particular, it is hard to avoid the over-used word 'intensity'.

This book presents the first English translation of Tsvetaeva's
Phaedra, written in 1926–27 (published in 1928), as well as three of her
'long poems',[8] written in the same two years. The poems are related to
the drama in impulse and aspiration, and all four works were created in
close biographical and emotional connection with her correspondence
with Rainer Maria Rilke (1875–1926) and Boris Pasternak (1890–1960).
Altogether the 1920s were for Tsvetaeva a time not only of poetic inspiration and creation but also of inspired letter-writing, especially to those
two other poets, with both of whom she was in love – at a distance: she
had left Russia and now lived in Paris, Pasternak had stayed in Moscow
after the Revolution, and Rilke was living in Switzerland. Her feelings
for both of them were indirectly expressed in her creative work.

The decade of the 1920s saw the creation of cycle after cycle of lyric
poems,[9] as well as three uniquely successful long poems in folk idiom[10]
and a series of other long poems which have received general admiration. 'Poem of the Mountain' and 'Poem of the End' were written in
1924 and published in 1926 (the latter shaking Pasternak to the core
– 'What a diabolically great artist you are, Marina!'[11] – and making
him rethink his idea of genius); 1926 also brought publication of *The
Ratcatcher*, written a year earlier, a work in which a contemporary critic

noted 'Rabelaisian vitality and inexhaustible verve'[12] and which, sixty years later, was still being described as a 'dazzlingly brilliant poem: her magnum opus');[13] then in 1926–27 came the three long poems presented in this book, 'Attempt at a Room', 'New Year's Letter' and 'Poem of the Air' (the first two published in 1928, the last in 1930). Equally talented as a prose writer, Tsvetaeva wrote numerous literary and autobiographical essays, most of the best of them in the 1930s. This is prose in which the voice of a poet can always be heard, instinctively avoiding cliché, interrogating language for its rhythms, sounds, connotations and etymologies, pushing it to produce more than its obvious aesthetic and semantic meanings.

Does her strong focus on the 'word as such' make Tsvetaeva a 'modernist' writer? She certainly lived and worked in the so-called modernist period and she was close, in innovative spirit, in genius, and to some extent biographically, to the best of the Russian poets some-times classified as 'modernist': Mayakovsky, Mandelstam, Akhmatova, Pasternak. Her recurrent motif of ascent may link her to Mandelstam's 'Acmeist' declaration that 'we do not fly, we ascend only those towers which we ourselves are able to build.'[14] But her difference from her contemporaries is greater than her similarity (as can indeed be said of each of them in relation to the others). She might seem to belong to the age through the remarkability of language itself in her work: the unusual foregrounding of rhythm, the verbal solidity and the sense that words might, if brilliantly handled, lead to the revelation of something unprecedented. Yet many features of 'modernism', such as a deliberate break with cultural tradition and rejection of history, do not seem to apply to Tsvetaeva; and the stylistic fragmentations and dislocations associated with it seem to me to have, in her case, little to do with the spirit of the age and everything to do with her own individual way of thinking. Tsvetaeva joined no group or movement and did not go in for experimenting or any kind of programmatic innovation. As for *Phaedra*, one could indeed point out that this work contains radical overturning of some traditions, for example the characters of the Nurse and of Phaedra, yet it also quietly follows many others, such as the basic story and many aspects of structure and dialogue. A deliberate stylistic dislocation may be felt in the juxtaposing of princely speech with folkloric diction, yet there Tsvetaeva may have been following what she knew of classical Greek tragedy, in which such mixing of levels is frequently found.[15] Her *Phaedra* is as recognisable and moving an example of tragic drama as any tragedies known to us, in particular the great previous treatments of the Phaedra legend: the *Hippolytus* of Euripides, Seneca's *Phaedra* and Racine's *Phèdre*.

'Every character – a torch of flame': I found myself thinking these words when I finished reading Tsvetaeva's *Phaedra* for the first time, and I continue to find a flame-like quality throughout it. The young huntsmen of scene one are fiery in their worship of Artemis, as is Hippolytus in his attachment to his misandrous mother; Phaedra is, explicitly, inflamed with love; her Nurse becomes kindled by the same flame; a servant, describing battle, expresses an inner heat of his own; Hippolytus's ardent hatred of secrecy is fanned by Phaedra's revelation of the single, too burning, secret he wants left unrevealed; even the two messengers are people of warmth; behind the cold, bull-bearing sea that destroys his son rages the hot anger of Theseus; the Nurse's confession is a last flaring up of emotional fire before the drama comes to an abruptly cooled conclusion.

Why is fiery intensity of feeling so highly valued that a whole drama is filled with it? Probably because, at least for Tsvetaeva, it is the best thing in our life and a unique means of gaining knowledge. A note she made in 1921 shows her identifying a high point of feeling with a 'correct seeing' of the world: rapture, or exaltation, as a condition for grasping what is true. 'Only at the peak of exaltation', she wrote, 'does a human being see the world correctly. God created the world in exaltation [. . .] a human being who is *not* in a state of exaltation cannot have a correct vision of things.'[16] The word here being translated as 'exaltation' is *vostorg*, often translated 'rapture'. To feel enraptured, rapt, seized, possessed, and to feel exalted, lifted up emotionally, raised on high by great longing or striving – these were, for Tsvetaeva, ways of describing similar experiences. When she wrote about poetic creation, she spoke of being possessed – ravished or enraptured. 'The condition of creation is a condition of entrancement. Until you begin – *obsession*, until you finish – *possession*'[17] (she uses French words here). The word *vostorg* in the 1921 note could just as well be rendered as 'rapture', yet both the accompanying 'peak' (*vershina*) and the word *vostorg* itself also suggest an ascent, climbing or being carried up to a height. The strength of the erotic, as well as the anti-erotic, feeling that fills this drama is related to that exaltation which the poet guessed was God's feeling in creating the world, and which she relates to human 'seeing correctly'. There is nothing sentimental in her conception of intense feeling. It is the conception not of an indulgence but of a force.

The three long poems included in the present book resemble the drama through the value given to a high peak of feeling, and in two of them the central image is that of an ascent. 'Poem of the Air' narrates a deliberate movement into something unimaginably high, leaving behind house and garden, earth altogether, and finally all traces of air. 'New Year's Letter' addresses someone who has already reached an unimaginably high place not even bounded by the concept of a god but having terrace upon terrace of gods: 'Must be more than one god there, and higher /up, another?' The concern with upward movement in these poems is not due to the sheer excitement of it, let alone to the pleasure of being above the rest of the world. It has all the force of discovering what is real.

Tsvetaeva is less known as a dramatist than as a poet. While still in Moscow, however, in 1918–19, she composed nine verse dramas, dedicated to individual actors of the Vakhtangov theatre,[18] with which she was then enthralled. None was performed but six are extant[19] – short, stylised, Romantic pieces set in the 16th–18th centuries. In 1923, after leaving Russia, she again turned to writing drama, this time finding her subjects in classical Greek myth, and working very fast: she was already thinking out a detailed plan for *Phaedra* while composing the play which preceded it, *Ariadne*. She wrote *Phaedra* between September 1926 and December 1927, spending a period of between five and eleven weeks on each of its four scenes. It was conceived as the second part of a dramatic trilogy of which the overall title, 'Theseus', supplanted an original title, 'The Rage of Aphrodite'. The three parts were to be 'Ariadne' (about Theseus as a young man), 'Phaedra' (with Theseus in middle age) and 'Helen' (his old age). The third was never written, and Tsvetaeva wrote no more plays.

There are several allusions in *Phaedra* to the legend on which *Ariadne* is based – the story of how the hero Theseus slays the Minotaur, marries the Cretan princess Ariadne and yields her to the god Dionysus. This more conventionally classical drama, with formal choruses and with gods appearing in person on the stage, contains some very fine verse and great lyrical moments, but is far less powerful than *Phaedra*, which is pruned of gods, formal choruses and intricacies of plot down to an essential clash of feelings and world-views.

The legend of Phaedra and Hippolytus

Phaedra,* daughter of King Minos and Pasiphaë, and wife of King **Theseus** of Athens, falls in love with her husband's son (by the Amazon queen **Antiope**) **Hippolytus**, who hates women, cultivates chastity and spends his time hunting in the forest and worshipping chaste **Artemis** – goddess of, *inter alia*, hunting and the moon. Phaedra falls ill from her illicit and secret desire, but her **Nurse** gets her to confess it to her, and persuades her to write Hippolytus a love-letter, Theseus being away on a journey. Phaedra takes this advice, is rejected by Hippolytus, and commits suicide. Theseus returns to find his wife dead, with a note in her hand accusing Hippolytus of raping her, or in another version, with the Nurse making this accusation; believing it, he calls on **Poseidon**, god of the sea, to destroy his son. News soon comes that, as Hippolytus was driving off in his chariot, a huge bull came out of the sea and his terrified horses dragged him to a ghastly death.

Related narratives relevant to Tsvetaeva's drama

Although known as the son of **Aegeus**, king of Athens, Theseus had the right to regard Poseidon as his father too, and to call on him for help. This was because the bed of his mother, Aethra (daughter of Pittheus, king of Troezen), had been visited during the same night by both Aegeus and Poseidon. Theseus grew up in Troezen (a city-state not far from Athens), was reunited with Aegeus and performed many valiant deeds, especially the killing of the Minotaur.

The Minotaur – half-man, half-bull – was born to **Pasiphaë** after she fell in love with a bull and contrived to copulate with it by concealing herself in the wooden replica of a cow. King Minos, her husband, imprisoned her monstrous offspring in a labyrinth in his palace at Cnossus, and compelled the Athenians to send seven girls and seven youths, every ninth year, to Crete to be devoured by it. On the third occasion of this horrible feasting, young Theseus nobly joined the group of youths to be sacrificed (or, in another version, was one of those chosen by lot). He killed the Minotaur and got out of the labyrinth by following a magic thread given him by **Ariadne** (daughter of Minos and Pasiphaë) who had fallen in love with him. He married Ariadne but left her on the island of Dia, later named Naxos, birthplace of the god

---

* Names in bold face are of characters who appear, or are mentioned, in Tsvetaeva's drama.

Dionysus/Bacchus; the god married her. Some say he forced Theseus to give her up.

One episode in Theseus's life was his abduction of the queen of the Amazons, Antiope (also known as Hippolyta), though some versions say she willingly joined his ship after his visit to her country. In any case, improbably enough, she fell in love with him and their union produced a son, Hippolytus. Improbably, because the Amazons, a female-only nation of warriors who each burned off one breast so as to use their weapons more easily, were known for their hatred of men. The Amazons waged war on the Athenians for abducting their queen, and Antiope died fighting at Theseus's side in the battle against her own people. But another version of the story is that she survived that battle and, when Theseus married Phaedra, she burst in, fully armed, on his wedding festivities, intending to massacre the guests; so Theseus was compelled to kill her.

After marrying Phaedra, Theseus sent his bastard infant son Hippolytus to Troezen, where Pittheus adopted him as heir to the Troezen throne. Here Hippolytus built a temple to the virginal Artemis, thereby enraging the goddess of erotic love, **Aphrodite**, who, to punish him, caused his stepmother Phaedra to fall in love with him.

Tsvetaeva's version of the legend

Scene one. Hippolytus's young huntsmen-friends chant of the 'absolute happiness' of their life in the forest, their worship of Artemis and total rejection of women, marriage, family and domesticity. They are loved by the gods, who admire youth and adventure. Artemis they see as virginal, vegetational, stone-hearted, a speeding vision always just out of sight; and Hippolytus they praise as her closest friend, the boldest of huntsmen, the most free from sexual bonds.

They drink and feast after a successful hunt. Hippolytus does not join the feast because of a disturbing dream in which he is visited by the one woman he loves, his mother, Antiope. Adorer of a goddess whom only trees are permitted to behold naked, he sees the dream-mother open her shroud to reveal breast and wound (the burnt-away right breast of the Amazon, or the arrow-wound that killed her?). When the vision disappears in smoke and steam, he lies helpless in the dream as if slain.

What is it he tries in vain to grasp amid the 'silence's utter thunder'– the breast? the wound? his origin? some essence of femaleness? Much of the drama's action has to do with keeping and revealing secrets.

Artemis's concealment of herself from the young hunters is a welcome secrecy to them, while Hippolytus's dream of the near-naked maternal body is a secret he does wish to grasp, even though in the dream his mother lifts her finger to her lips as if to prevent enquiry.

His friends remind him what life is really about: not female mysteries but wine, laughter, youth, sport, men without women. At this moment Phaedra appears, lost in the forest, and sees Hippolytus for the first time.

Scene two. In her palace Phaedra lies ill and unconscious, that one glimpse of Hippolytus having inflamed her with desire for him. She raves of the myrtle tree (symbol of love), and of thundering horse-hooves and heavy fruit in a tree – omens of Hippolytus's death and of her own. Her maidservants are bewildered. Her Nurse (once wetnurse, now servant and companion) recalls how she journeyed with her from Athens to Troezen, and how Phaedra, seeing the dense forests there, rushed headlong into them (unwittingly betraying, we may think, an affinity with the huntsmen, whose opening cry 'O thickets!' could be hers too) – to emerge from the forest, later, strangely 'changed'. When Phaedra wakes, the Nurse recounts the unhappy fates of Pasiphaë and Ariadne, and with much persistence gets her to confess she is unhappy as Theseus's third wife, strongly agreeing that she ought indeed to be unhappy: 'Phaedra, they mated you with a spider!'

Practically all of scene two consists in the gradual uncovering of secrets. Phaedra's is revealed in two stages – first that she is in love with someone other than her husband; then that her beloved is her husband's son. But the Nurse, too, has a secret and, while persuading Phaedra to speak out, she reveals it, again in two stages. First comes her belief that she has a special elemental closeness to Phaedra. Then comes her hope that she herself, a servant deprived of any love-life, will vicariously enjoy Phaedra's love-making with Hippolytus. Her powerfully released language of desire sweeps away Phaedra's horrified objections to planning an immediate meeting with Hippolytus 'in the woods'. As the Nurse's rhetoric intensifies, Phaedra weakens and is persuaded to write Hippolytus a letter.

Scene three. After the preceding scene's absorption in the longings of two women, one young and one old, this shorter scene opens with a greatly contrasting but no less profoundly emotional dialogue of two men – one young, one old. An unnamed servant describes to the eager Hippolytus how his mother died at his father's side in the battle against her own people, the Amazons. The detail of how the arc of her bow resembles her missing breast must recall Hippolytus's dream in scene one, so the account of the battle here is like a second dream of his mother.

Just as the Nurse worked hard to get Phaedra to speak of her love, now the servant tries hard to persuade Hippolytus to give up his insistence on chastity. Sexual love, he claims, is like a baby's suckling: to neither does resistance last long. This coincides with the Nurse's unexpected arrival, in which the same two motifs (sex and milk) are combined, for she enters repeating her conviction about the universal power of milk, at the same time handing to Hippolytus the love letter from Phaedra. Seeing the inscription, 'secret', he smashes the clay tablet and utters a soliloquy against everything secretive, maintaining that the only things that should be hidden are monsters and lechery. 'Except for lechery' – these words turn out to be the kernel of the matter, for Phaedra now enters, 'her finger to her lips' (like the mother in the dream), at once keeping her secret and ready to reveal it. In the ensuing dialogue, the high-point of this play, queen speaks to prince, woman to woman-hater, stepmother to stepson, eros to anti-eros, a person entranced and loving to one who is sober and hostile. Tsvetaeva jotted in her notebook that she meant Phaedra to be '*beyond* transgression', 'a young woman madly in love, deeply understandable', who '*speaks as if in her sleep*, therefore not hearing his exclamations; then she comes to her senses, slain by his answer.'[20] As Hippolytus reached out to his dream-mother but met only smoke and steam, now his stepmother reaches out to him and meets only rejection.

Scene four.[21] Phaedra has hanged herself from the myrtle tree. The grieving Nurse resolves to save at least Phaedra's honour by telling Theseus that in his absence she was persecuted by the lustful behaviour of his son. Returning, Theseus is told the false tale and calls on the sea-god Poseidon to make good his long-ago promise by destroying Hippolytus. A messenger brings news of Hippolytus's death: a great bull from the sea maddened his horses, which dragged him to his death. The young huntsmen from scene one reappear, to mourn him. The maidens, however, refuse to lament Phaedra's death and instead speak of her courage, advising all women boldly to seek their desire.

This scene is again largely built on the revelation of secrets. A servant bringing the fragments of the tablet (the love-letter) marks the beginning of an 'openness' (as if in honour of Hippolytus's scene three monologue): Phaedra's guilt is revealed and the Nurse reveals her own role in what has happened. Theseus, now accepting the truth, does not attend to the 'stupid old woman'. Instead he makes a reconciliatory speech: we are mere tools in the hands of the gods, who fight their own battles through us – thus 'a / *poor* woman's love for a *poor* young child – is / Aphrodite's hatred of me'. He states that Phaedra and Hippolytus should be buried (uncomfortably, one may imagine) in a single grave.

Characters

Tsvetaeva's Phaedra is presented as wholly innocent. It is clear she is possessed by an elemental force she cannot reject, yet also clear that she would not have acted on her desire but for the urgings of the Nurse. She is presented as young, not at all as someone approaching middle age. She has no children (although the traditional legend gives her two) and she makes no speeches of wisdom. She is said to go running like an adolescent into the forests of Troezen, and she is timid. When starting to speak to Hippolytus, in scene three, she could be a shy schoolgirl confessing to her teacher a helpless adoration.

Some details recall the Phèdre of Racine. The semi-delirious 'Full-gallop you'll go flying past. / Down to you I shall lean from the bough' (scene two) recalls the earlier Phèdre's 'Dieux! Que ne suis-je assise à l'ombre des forêts! Quand pourrai-je, au travers d'une noble poussière, Suivre de l'œil un char fuyant dans la carrière?'[22] But Racine's heroine is a mature, queenly woman who speaks of her children, is aware of royal politics, is shocked by her own guilty passion and is able to be cruel – making Hippolytus's life miserable with her pretence of hating him, agreeing that Theseus be told the lie about his son, and blaming Oenone (her 'Nurse') for the consequent disaster. Tsvetaeva's Phaedra has no previous acquaintance with Hippolytus and there is no trace of hate in her love for him; she obeys and trusts her Nurse after her one cry of 'Bawd!' Of course she plays no part in telling the lie to Theseus – it is told after her death. Nor does Tsvetaeva invent any equivalent to Aricie, with whom Racine's Hippolyte, no longer committed to chastity, is in love – unthinkable for Tsvetaeva's Ippolìt. Racine's Phèdre is jealous of Aricie; Tsvetaeva's is jealous of no one and blames no one.

Hippolytus, too, seems very young in this drama. Where Racine gives him the rationality and urbane manners of someone older, Tsvetaeva shows him surrounded by bold young hunters, festive drinkers, despisers of urban proprieties; his home is a 'lair'. As if to a youth, older men give him advice (servants in scenes one and three), none of which he heeds. Polite at first to the visiting stepmother-queen, when she challenges his deepest convictions his retort is blurted and barbaric.

Further, while Phaedra is always presented in dialogue, Hippolytus is characterised mainly through four monologues, which variously point to paradoxes. His last long speech in scene three, for example, praises 'openness' at the very moment when he is about to destroy an important letter which he refuses to open. He attacks secrecy, but keeps secret from himself the whole nature of the erotic. Tsvetaeva has created a new, more complex and interesting version of Hippolytus.

The Nurse, traditionally an important minor character, is here even more important. In scene two she speaks well over three times more lines than Phaedra does. If Phaedra is possessed by passionate love, and Hippolytus by the determination to avoid it, the Nurse is – or becomes – fixated on the thought of the erotic as such. When she finds out that Phaedra's illness is due to love, she begins speaking of an 'ancestral woe', a 'certain power' which once 'hurtled down' from above and without which humans would not exist. At the very end of the drama she virtually identifies herself with that power: 'Flog, but know, / in this place / I'm the gods.' Between those two moments she evolves from benevolent servant into a person obsessed with a bodily relationship (of infant and wetnurse) which has strong sexual implications. To the revelation that Phaedra is in love with her own stepson she responds with sheer satisfaction – the antithesis of her response in Euripides, Seneca and Racine. She immediately plans a rendezvous in the woods, just as if she herself were going to it: 'lips to lips! – Today! At once!' In her increasingly sensual language there is even an element of the vampiric. This becomes quasi-explicit when she says: 'I'm / feeding on your youth, as once – / sweet hours! – you used to feed on mine.' After which she becomes temporarily incoherent, as if she, too, is crazed with desire.

Two years before she started writing *Phaedra*, Tsvetaeva wrote the long poem 'Mólodets' (the only long work she dedicated to Pasternak). Usually translated as 'The Swain', it is based on the Russian folk tale 'The Vampire'.[23] The peasant girl Marusya falls in love with a strange young man she meets at a village dance, and does not reject him even when she comes upon him eating a corpse in a church. So as not to lose him, she sacrifices to him her parents, her brother and, finally, herself – upon all of whom he *feeds*. A significant alteration Tsvetaeva made to the folk story is that in her version the vampire, associated with the element of fire, is not evil; he tries to save his victims. If Marusya would say openly what she saw in the church, she and her family would be free of him, and he begs her to do so; but she is possessed by love and refuses to say it. Neither is the Nurse in *Phaedra* evil, despite all the wrong she does and dreams of. Another connecting-point with *Phaedra* is that 'The Swain' is written in the diction of folk poetry and folk tales; similarly, Phaedra's Nurse often speaks in a folkish dialect (see *Rhythms* below).

Comparisons

Tsvetaeva once claimed that the source for her planned dramatic trilogy was the popular 19th-century account of classical myths by Gustav Schwab, but she also stated that its real sources were within herself. She knew Euripides, probably Seneca and certainly Racine. All the same she presents the mythical characters very much in her own way. Here are some brief comparisons, scene by scene, with earlier Phaedra dramas.

Scene one. No deity is represented in Tsvetaeva's drama, whereas Euripides starts with Aphrodite announcing her plan to punish Hippolytus for scorning her, and ends with Artemis blaming Aphrodite for all that has gone wrong. Tsvetaeva's huntsmen do speak as a sort of chorus, but there is no regular classical Chorus here such as in Euripides and Seneca. The opening of Tsvetaeva's drama slightly resembles that of Seneca's: there, too, is a hunting scene with hills, thickets, boars and praise of Diana (the Greek Artemis), though with Hippolytus allocating tasks and territories to his fellow huntsmen. In Euripides, too, near the beginning, the huntsmen offer praise to Artemis. But Hippolytus's dream and Phaedra's chancing upon him in the forest are Tsvetaeva's additions.

Scene two. The lovesick Phaedra's illness and confusion, and her Nurse's and maidservants' bewilderment, are traditional subject-matter; similarly, the to-and-fro dialogue, in which the Nurse gradually discovers who Phaedra is in love with, has counterparts in Euripides, Seneca and Racine. But the 'haunted third-wife' motif, greatly played on by Tsvetaeva's persuasive Nurse, is new, and both the Nurse's lactal philosophy and her involvement in Phaedra's erotic life are also Tsvetaeva's innovations. Euripides has his sympathetic Nurse declare: 'What you want / is not fine words, but the man!' [24] but there is no sign that she might want the same thing. Racine's Oenone stresses that she has given up her own life to attend Phèdre ('Mon pays, mes enfants, pour vous j'ai tout quitté')[25] and is so attached to Phèdre that she kills herself when she is rejected; but her feelings spring from devotion and self-sacrifice. The vicarious-erotic motif is unique to Tsvetaeva.

Scene three. The servant here may be seen as something of a *confidant*, like Racine's Théramène. But Hippolytus's speeches about Antiope's death and his own inevitable childlessness are additions to the traditional treatment of the legend. However, his speech in praise of 'openness' resembles the one Euripides's Hippolytus makes (to the Nurse) about a pure world without women; it also resembles the one in Seneca about honesty and a wholesome woodland life.

There are big differences in the ways Hippolytus learns of Phaedra's love. In Euripides, the Nurse tells him, with the eavesdropping Phaedra crying 'I am destroyed for ever!'[26] In Seneca, while the Nurse is trying to persuade him to give up his vow of chastity, Phaedra enters, swooning, and, being gathered up in his filially unsuspecting arms, shocks him by declaring her love. In Racine's drama, Phèdre, talking to Hippolyte, lets the confession slip out inadvertently. Only in Tsvetaeva's does Phaedra herself intentionally declare her love to Hippolytus, hoping to win him over. Something like Phaedra's narrative of the history of her love also occurs in Euripides, Seneca and Racine, but (once again) it is only in Tsvetaeva's version that Phaedra tells it directly to her beloved.

Scene four. Though with different emphases, this final scene largely follows the classical legend. Phaedra's suicide, Theseus's return, his ready belief in the false tale (here told by the Nurse, not by Phaedra), his curse upon his son, the messenger's detailed account of Hippolytus's death, the final revealing of the truth and Theseus's concluding speech – all these elements are present in Euripides, Seneca and Racine. Tsvetaeva's Nurse's speeches and actions here, however, have no counterpart in the earlier dramas.

The description of Hippolytus's death is very much a set-piece in these early Phaedra dramas, the details being the same in them all, as well as in the account by Ovid. But Tsvetaeva's version of it is remarkable for being very much more concise, while as vivid and harrowing. Its brevity leaves room for the greater sadness about Phaedra.

Tsvetaeva's play ends differently from the preceding ones. Euripides's Hippolytus, on whom his attention has been more focused than on Phaedra, is brought back terribly wounded and forgives his lamenting father with his dying breath. Seneca's is brought back, too, as a mangled corpse, and Theseus utters words of reconcilement. Racine has Phèdre die of poison in the presence of her husband, whose final short speech, after an unforgiving word about her 'action si noire', is of grief and guilt towards his son. Tsvetaeva alone concludes the drama, if somewhat mechanically, with general forgiveness and submission to the will of the gods.

Another earlier treatment of the legend which deserves mention is the 1864 dramatic fragment 'Phaedra' by Algernon Charles Swinburne. Tsvetaeva did not read English and may not have known Swinburne's work, despite his being for a while Pasternak's favourite English poet. This seven-page dialogue consists mainly of speeches by Phaedra who, with Hippolytus's sword in her hand, demands that he kill her – a wish uttered also in the dramas of Racine and Seneca, but radically transmuted by Tsvetaeva into a proposal that the two of them should die together. Swinburne has some images similar to Tsvetaeva's, as in his fine line 'The bright writing of my name is black', which resembles the Russian Phaedra's mentioning her own name, implying its meaning of 'bright'. 'My name is Phaedra', she says in scene two, a phrase I have translated as 'My name means "shining"'. Swinburne's love-language includes both 'feeding on' the beloved (Tsvetaeva's Nurse's language) and being 'burnt' by love (her Phaedra's):

> Thou art my son, I am thy father's wife,
> I ache toward thee with a bridal blood,
> The pulse is heavy in all my married veins,
> My whole face beats, I will feed full of thee,
> My body is empty of ease, I will be fed,
> I am burnt to the bone with love . . .[27]

The passionateness in Swinburne's lines is very like that in Tsvetaeva's, but the demanding, even commanding, figure he creates has little in common with the tender youthfulness of Tsvetaeva's Phaedra.

Rhythms

While working on scene three of *Phaedra*, Tsvetaeva told Pasternak how vital its rhythms were to her: '. . . nothing depends on me. It is all a matter of the rhythm I shall fall into. My lines are carried by the rhythm, as my words are by the voice into which I fall. As soon as I'm in the wrong rhythm (and what is the *right* one? all I know is – not *this* one!),[28] everything is over, three lines a day, not just winglessness – pawlessness. In a word, one minute it carries me, the next I am crawling.'[29] A year previously, Pasternak found in *The Ratcatcher*, her 'lyrical satire' of 1925, 'the absolute and undivided supremacy of rhythm'.[30] Something similar might be said of *Phaedra*. It is a highly aural drama, written in energetic, inventive, provocative verse tensely controlled by rhymes and rhythms. New metrical patterns are introduced, one after another, to be repeated with great consistency as well as great flexibility. Strict forms unite with a natural freedom. It is interesting that two prominent émigré writers who, upon the publication of *Phaedra* in 1928, fiercely criticised it for what they saw as its unacceptable mixture of styles, also wrote of its extraordinarily 'enchanting' use of rhythm.[31]

I have not reflected the poet's use of rhyme in my translation as it would have caused too much distortion of meaning. (On rhyme, see 'Translating *Phaedra*'.) But I have reproduced the original's line-lengths and tried to approximate its predominant metres. Below, I hope to give an idea of the unusualness and brilliance of Tsvetaeva's verse to readers who have only this translation to go by. The Nurse's style of speaking is most interesting of all, while being, alas, the most untranslatable.

Many lines are very short – dimetric or trimetric; none longer than tetrameter. The commonest foot is the trochee (/ x). Often one senses a regular beat of / x / x / x / x , perhaps suggestive of the heavy heartbeat of Phaedra delirious, or of the heartbeats of all the characters, driven as they are by emotion and doom, or perhaps of the fatal horse-hooves Phaedra hears in her sleep. Also typical are amphibrach (x / x), choriamb (/ x x /), dactyl (/ x x) – metres which, with the trochee, are the most common in Russian folk poems. Lines combining two or more specific metres ('logaoedic' lines)[32] or able to be scanned in more than one way, often occur as well. The opening line: '*O zárosl*'! *O zov*!' – echoed in the translation as 'O thickets! O cry!' – scans best as amphibrach-plus-iambus (x / x + x /) but identical arrangements of stresses elsewhere scan better as iambus-plus-anapaest (x / + x x /) or as monosyllable-plus-choriamb (x + / x x /). These three scansion possibilities occur, in the original, throughout the first sixty lines of scene four (Nurse's lament and resolve), where despite their astounding variety each one of the sixty can be charted as: x / x x /.

This metrical pattern is used for sixteen or so lines in the huntsmen's opening choruses, where occasionally my English lines repeat it, as in the opening line quoted above and line two of stanza eight: '*Prokhláda. Privál*', 'A coolness. A halt'.

For rhythm, the most noteworthy scene is the second. Phaedra's way of speaking is vividly distinguished from that of Nurse and maids. She speaks mainly in trochaic tetrameters while the servants use a looser style, echoing traditional Russian folk poems with their irregular stress-patterns and their many lines ending in a dactyl or even hyperdactyl (three unstressed syllables): this has the effect of a slipping into a kind of singing or muttering. Nurse and maids are further distinguished from

Phaedra in using archaic and folkloric words and many folk-style word-contractions and expansions: Tsvetaeva knew Russian folk poetry well and was expert at creating variants of it. According to Brodsky, 'of the entire pleiad of great twentieth-century Russian poets, with the exception of Nikolay Klyuyev, Tsvetaeva stands closest to folklore'.[33] The poet Vladislav Khodasevich,[34] though often critical of her work (as he was, in fact, of *Phaedra*), expressed unqualified admiration for her imitation of Russian folk-verse in 'The Swain'.[35] Her ease with the folkloric can be seen in the diction she creates for Phaedra's Nurse.

All this is thoroughly daunting to the translator! Easier to render are the quoting of apparent proverbs, such as: 'Know the illness – know the balm', and the habit of counting things in threes, as in 'I've scoured three hills' or of using three verbs for one ('we'll hide it, bury it, trample it').

But the most striking feature of the Nurse's speech is an idiosyncratic four-line metrical figure which contributes to revealing a witch-like dimension in her personality. This 'four-line chant', as I shall call it, is used twenty-seven times, and only by the Nurse, except when Phaedra's short interruptions continue it. It first appears in scene two at the line 'All that suckling and all that feeding you', and it scans as follows: first line – / x / x x / x / x x ; second line the same); third drops the two final non-stresses) – / x / x x / x /; fourth is suddenly short – / x / x /. My translation sometimes gets close to this. Here are three consecutive four-line chants from the Nurse's speech in scene two about Phaedra's unlucky lot in being a third wife. The first two quatrains (occurring in continuous, unseparated lines) are an approximation to the original's pattern, the last one shows it exactly.

> Phaedra, they mated you with a spider!
> Take revenge on him, give up make-believe,
> you're not guilty in any way.
> Into your husband's house
>
> you came, a late-coming wife, the third of them.
> Two wives met with the new young wife at the
> threshold, two wives not of this earth
> led the young one in.
>
> 'Here', they said to her, 'live, enjoy yourself',
> took the younger one's hands and guided her.
> Phaedra, all of your nights and days
> pass beneath their shade.

The long speech which contains these quatrains mentions a number of uncanny phenomena – ghosts, curses, the evil eye (serpents' eyes), a bewitched bed. And yet it is, above all, the Nurse's language, her use of verbal rhythms and especially of the incantatory four-liner, that make for a sinister effect. It seems that, while lamenting another's curse, she herself lays a curse upon Phaedra.

Meanwhile Phaedra, who at one point could say 'Old woman, how you prattle on', falls under the spell of these strange metres and of the Nurse's witch-like repetitions. Examples of the latter: '*Znáyu, chúyu, vízhu, slýshu*' (I know, I sense, I see, I hear), and, towards the end of scene two: '*Skróyem, vróyem, vtópchem styd* ' ('We'll hide, we'll bury, we'll trample shame' – translated as 'bury and hide and trample the shame'). The poet thoroughly exploits the repetitive endings of Russian verbs and the language's ability to do without personal pronouns, all of which reinforces the effect of a powerful enchantment. All these examples, moreover, are strongly trochaic, a mode which English with its unavoidable monosyllables (I, you, we, a, the) tends to weaken into iambics.

There is a significant difference between the language of Theseus and that of the Nurse, who both cause the death of one they love. Upright Theseus, to destroy his son, eloquently calls upon the god of the sea, using heroic-sounding archaisms, while the now half-crazily chanting Nurse calls up uncanny forces lurking in demotic speech. Phaedra's death is not her intention, but her three lines closing scene two imply that death is not too high a price for what she has in mind.

> Laurel-walnut-almond!
> Upon a goodly tree
> no shame to hang yourself!

When she comes to the fore in the final scene, the contrast with Theseus is strongly marked. Except for one marvellous speech in her former half-dactylic folk-style, she is reduced, now blaming herself for everything, to a stuttering two-stress line:

> Bull and bough,
> corpse and corpse –
> work of these hands,
> work of these lips.
> [...]

Theseus, by contrast, speaks in stately tetrameters as he shifts all responsibility onto the gods:

> Hippolytus' horses and Phaedra's bough aren't
> old woman's intrigues, they're ancient knockings
> of fate. Can human beings shift mountains?
> [...]
> In different form, and in different fashion,
> still the same guilt is being punished.
> New lightning, old thundercloud.

Poetry in correspondence with Pasternak and Rilke

Although Tsvetaeva had met Pasternak in Moscow, it was only after her emigration, when it was practically impossible for them to meet, that they discovered each other as poets and as persons. In 1922–23 her love for Pasternak was all-consuming, as was her disappointment when he returned to Moscow from a visit to Berlin, thereby giving up any chance of their meeting. This disappointment led her to write, in 1923, ten very powerful poems addressed to him.[36] 'Non-meetings' are a theme central to two long poems, 'Attempt at a Room' and 'New Year's Letter', and they are echoed in Phaedra's virtual non-meeting with Hippolytus. Through Pasternak, Tsvetaeva became acquainted with Rilke; her subsequent correspondence with him during 1926 was as impassioned and sincere as that with Pasternak. Indeed, the urgency with which, in many of her letters, she expressed her thoughts about poetry, and about both Pasternak and Rilke as poets, is germane to the general atmosphere of *Phaedra*, albeit this drama is directly concerned with erotic love rather than with art.

The strange and difficult poem 'Attempt at a Room', written in June 1926, belongs to the complex relationship she had with the two poets whom she loved but could not meet. It sets out to construct – or, in some wilful and exalted way, to *be* – a room, a four-walled space in which two poets' minds can meet for a non-bodily yet blissful version of a lovers' meeting. The poem shares with *Phaedra* this theme of an attempt to bring about a perfect, almost otherworldly, meeting with someone loved and intangible. The quasi-physical constructing of the room is described, off and on, throughout the poem, and when in the end the room collapses, there paradoxically remain the 210 lines of the metrically highly regular, thus very noticeably *constructed*, literary work, with its unspoken idea that *it* is the intended room, somehow a real opportunity for meeting. At first the poet notionally invited to the room of the poem was Pasternak. At Rilke's death, however, it was rededicated to Rilke, despite its references to Pasternak's youthful piano-playing and to two dreams, one of them a dream Pasternak had had and mentioned to Tsvetaeva, the other a dream which, in an earlier poem, she imagines him having about her. In January 1927 she wrote to Pasternak: 'Shuddering, I realised that the poem about the two of us, "Attempt at a Room", is not about us but about . . .'[37] Her sentence is unfinished.

Letters exchanged between Tsvetaeva and Pasternak in the early 1920s show how close they felt they were, temperamentally and creatively. In one of his very first letters, in 1922, the statement, 'I know you love – to put it briefly – poetry, no less passionately than I do',[38] led to an exquisitely fine (if, for others, rather difficult to follow) explanation of what poetry meant to him. Two years later, as much in love with her as she was with him, he started a letter with: 'Marina, my golden friend, my amazing supernaturally kindred destiny, my smoky early-morning soul, Marina . . .'[39] Meanwhile, Tsvetaeva was writing drafts of her new poems on the very pages which held drafts of her letters to Pasternak. She told him about this: 'Letters to you I always write into my notebook, at speed, as the rough drafts of poems. Only, they don't become a fair copy: two rough drafts, one for you, one for me. You and poems [. . .] are for me inseparable. I don't need to come out of the poems in order to write to you, I write in you.'[40] And yet by 1926 Pasternak was already undergoing a change that was taking him away from her – away from lyric poetry and towards what he called 'historicism', a commitment to understanding the pains and concerns of the Soviet age and to doing something responsible in relation to them, starting with the composition of deliberately non-esoteric narrative poems on contemporary subjects. The shock and sorrow, for Tsvetaeva, of realising that he was moving into something which they no longer shared, and which she could not admire, had a remarkable effect on her writing of *Phaedra* – it gave her a kind of tragic energy, rather as his failure to meet up with her in 1923 had spurred her to compose a cycle of brilliant poems. She wrote to him, that August, that she was correcting part one of her dramatic trilogy and hoping to start on part two (meaning *Phaedra*): 'Now that I have such grief – *you* – I shall write well. Hippolytus will be not merely loved but loved-to-excess'.[41] The rest of this letter is full of her grief over Pasternak, and in subsequent letters she tried hard to persuade him to turn back to his original source of inspiration, writing again in August 1926:

> You are a lyric poet, Boris, such as the world has never before seen nor God created [. . .] Abandon plot, plot is beneath you [. . .] Don't have events. *Being* is eventless [. . .] You, when you write – you place the poem on the paper, in an instant, a single gesture, no first or last line. That's wholly what you are. You are entire, like an explosion. [. . .] Nothing will ever console me for the loss of you. . . [42]

Some six months later she still wrote in similar vein: 'Dear Boris, you are obviously, heroically, on the wrong path.'[43] At one point she thought he might be joining the Communist Party, 'the one thing that would separate us forever.'[44] Pasternak (who was far from joining the Party) countered with sadness, diffidence and pangs of hope for the revival of his former lyrical self, but also with such statements as: 'you underestimate certain serious aspects of me . . .' and 'I cannot possibly describe the moral hell and anguish in which I am seething here . . . I am suffocating in a sophistry which causes all genuine thoughts to disintegrate.'[45] The word 'history' had a different meaning for each of them. Tsvetaeva, in France, could say: 'For you there is history, for me – epic. One can master history, but one ENTERS epic like walking into a field of rye.'[46] But Pasternak, in Soviet Russia, felt that his response to the 'history' going on in his own time and place had to be a huge effort of mastering a new, plain, altruistic style. This change in him would eventually lead to the writing of what he called his 'novel in prose', *Doctor Zhivago*, begun five years after Tsvetaeva's death, and who knows whether he was recalling her lovely image of walking into a field of rye when, for the last line of the *Zhivago* poem 'Hamlet' he quoted the popular saying, 'Living a life is not walking across a field.'

Rilke, too, was an influence on her work, and, like Pasternak, a great spur to it. Not knowing how ill he was, she had been writing to him for some five months and had received six long, delighted letters from him, as well as an elegy addressed to her when, after a period of silence, she had the shock of learning that he had died, at the very end of 1926. His death, far from putting a stop to her side of the correspondence, led to its renewal: she now became so engrossed in writing to him that her work on *Phaedra* was interrupted for five months. But she wrote to him now in new ways: after one short, normal-looking letter, in German, dated 31 December,[47] there came a long piece of Russian prose entitled 'Your

Death',[48] then the two long poems of which translations are offered in the present volume. She mentioned the first of these to Pasternak in the very sentence in which she told him she had been writing *Phaedra*: 'I have been writing Part Two since the Autumn, but have broken it off with a letter to Rilke which I finished only yesterday (in anguish)'.[49] This 'letter' was the long poem 'New Year's Letter' of February 1927, which in part develops motifs from the letter of 31 December. In it she wishes Rilke a Happy New Year in the new place he now inhabits, imagines his journey to it, asks him what it is like, with other questions flowing from her at once buoyant and melancholy metaphysics. Despite lamenting that nothing ever came of their relationship, she puts forward her idea of poetry as a 'third thing' uniting life and death – an idea which recalls 'Attempt at a Room' with its wholly serious conception that a poem could be a place to meet in.

A little later in 1927 came the much longer 'Poem of the Air'. Spurred into being by Charles Lindbergh's solo flight across the Atlantic in May of that year, it mainly describes an imagined journey (guided apparently by an unnamed, ghostly Rilke), not across the sea but upward through seven ever sparser levels of air, to an ultimate, yet uncompleted, ecstatic condition. Of this work Tsvetaeva wrote to Pasternak in June: 'I am now writing something utterly lonely, isolating; I am terribly carried away'; and at the end of the same letter: 'Boris, I am writing something which will make your skin shiver. This work is the beginning of my solitude'.[50]

Scene three of *Phaedra* was begun two or three weeks after the completion of the skin-shivering 'Poem of the Air'; still, that is, in the aftermath of grief over Rilke and the related desire to rise to a higher level where inspired minds may meet. Although 'Poem of the Air' goes far beyond desire for a lover and seems to end in the positive solitude mentioned in the letters, it might be said that the bodily love which Phaedra offers to Hippolytus but which swerves, at almost the last moment of her last speech, upward (as it were) into a desire for eternal union with him in something like Heaven ('where no stepsons are, no stepmothers . . .') resembles the longing which informs the whole of 'Poem of the Air'.

With similar focus on eternity, Tsvetaeva told Pasternak, a while after this: 'I want to be with you for an hour which would last forever'.[51] No such hour ever came. Their correspondence lost warmth and closeness, and when they did at last meet, in 1935, it was in the most unfavourable circumstances imaginable: Pasternak, ill with depression and neuras-thenia, had been commanded to leave his sanatorium and travel to Paris to take part in the Second International Congress of Writers in Defence of Culture. His meetings with Tsvetaeva there were deeply disappointing to them both. Their few encounters between her return to the Soviet Union in 1939 and her suicide in 1941 seem scarcely connected with the extraordinary epistolary intimacy they had enjoyed for more than ten years.

In August 1927, while still trying to persuade Pasternak not to abandon his lyric genius, Tsvetaeva was writing the third scene of *Phaedra* with its great description of Antiope in battle. Although about fighting, this speech could well be seen as offering an analogy for the absorption and rapture of the creative process.

> Taking aim, not just with eye and
> elbow, but with every pulsing
> vein, aiming her whole aimed
> body, equal of men – no, equal
> of gods (her never-used-up quiver
> fuller than a horn of plenty),
> radiant under the foe's arrows,
> there she stood, afraid of nothing.

Again and again Tsvetaeva found words to express the supreme happiness of absorption in creation. In finding them she revealed unforeseen splendours of language. In the 1920s some of her critics found her style awkward or obscure, but others besides Pasternak already felt her power,[52] and since that time her fame has grown immensely: she is now loved and admired by large numbers of readers, both in Russia and in other countries. A Russian scholar said that whenever she came abroad to give readings of Tsvetaeva's poetry (in the 1990s and 2000s) she was astonished by the enthusiasm of her foreign audiences: 'Where do these burning eyes come from, in every town that I visit? Why do I see them again and again at my lectures?'[53] It is evident that, even in translation, what is able to come across is not just the poet's own passions and insights but, far more, that which she knew she shared with Rilke and with Pasternak: the passionate and insightful work with language, the pulsing veins of it, the fearlessness and the radiance.

Notes

(For full references see Further Reading)

1. M. Tsvetaeva, B. Pasternak, *Dushi nachinayut videt'. Pis'ma 1922-36 godov* [Souls Begin to See. Letters 1922-36; hereafter *Letters*], edited by E.B. Korkina and I.D. Shevelenko, Moscow, 2004, p. 184.

2. Brodsky, p. 191.

3. Mark Rudman, *Diverse Voices: Essays on Poets and Poetry*, Brownsville, OR, 1993, p. 225. (Emphasis - A.L.)

4. Irma Kudrova. *Prostory Mariny Tsvetaevoy. Poeziya, proza, lichnost'* [The spaces of Marina Tsvetaeva. Poetry, prose, personality], St Petersburg, 2003, p. 10.

5. Fazil Iskander, quoted in Kudrova, *Put' komet. Zhizn' Mariny Tsvetaevoy* [The Path of Comets. The Life of Marina Tsvetaeva], St Petersburg, 2002, p. 744.

6. Todorov, p. 11.

7. E.g. Brodsky, p. 188.

8. A long, narrative or discursive, poem is in Russian *poéma* (three syllables, plural *poémy*), translated in this book as 'long poem'.

9. *Versty* [Milestones], 1922; *Razluka* [Parting], 1922; *Stikhi k Bloku* [Poems to Blok], 1922; *Psikheya* [Psyche], 1923; *Remeslo* [Craft], 1923; *Posle Rossii* [After Russia], 1928.

10. *Tsar'-devitsa* [The Tsar-Maiden], 1922; *Pereulochki* [Side-streets], 1922; *Mólodets* [The Swain], 1924.

11. *Letters*, p. 149.

12. D.S. Mirsky in *New Statesman* XXVI, 27 February 1926; reprinted in Mirsky, *Uncollected Writings on Russian Literature*, edited by G.S. Smith, Berkeley CA, 1989, pp. 217-21.

13. Karlinsky, pp. 146, 180.

14. Osip Mandelstam, 'Utro Akmeizma' [The Morning of Acmeism], 1913, first published 1919. Mandel'shtam, *Sochineniya v dvukh tomakh* [Works in two volumes], II, edited by Averintsev and Nerler, Moscow, 1990, pp. 141–45.

15. Michael Makin writes convincingly about Tsvetaeva's closeness to classical tragedy. Makin, pp. 290–93.

16. *M. Tsvetaeva. Neizdannoye. Svodnyye tetradi* [M. Tsvetaeva. Unpublished material. Collated notebooks], edited by E.B. Korkina and I.D. Shevelenko, Moscow, 1997.

17. *Navazhdeniye* is translated 'entrancement' in ALC, p. 172.

18. Yevgeny Vakhtangov was the famous director, in the 1910s, of the 'Third Studio' at the Moscow Art Theatre, which was renamed the Vakhtangov Theatre after his death in 1922.

19. *Chervonnyy valet* [The Knave of Hearts], *Metel'* [Snowstorm], *Fortuna*, *Kamennyy angel* [The Stone Angel], *Priklyucheniye* [An Adventure], *Feniks* [Phoenix].

20. Notebook, quoted in *Sobraniye sochineniy v semi tomakh* [Collected Works in Seven Volumes], edited by Anna Saakyants and Lev Mnukhin, Moscow, 1994, vol. III, p. 807 (Tsvetaeva's emphasis).

21. A fifth scene, to be called 'Horses' and with emphasis on Hippolytus, was planned but was not written.

22. 'Ye gods! Would that I were seated in the shade of forests! When may I, through a noble dust, watch the full-speed flight of a chariot?' Racine, *Phèdre* (act 1, scene 3).

23. Tora Lane's *Rendering the Sublime, A Reading of Marina Tsvetaeva's Fairy-Tale Poem*

'*The Swain*', Stockholm, 2009 (including Russian text) describes and discusses the folk-language used in *Molodets*.

24. Euripides (translated by Grene), p. 183.

25. 'For you I left everything – my country, my children.' Racine, *Phèdre* (act 1, scene 3).

26. Euripides, p. 186.

27. Swinburne, p. 25, lines 64–69.

28. A similar moment is described in the essay 'Art in the Light of Conscience', ALC, p. 173.

29. *Letters*, p. 374.

30. *Letters*, p. 249.

31. Vladislav Khodasevich in the journal *Vozrozhdeniye*, 27 September 1928, and Georgy Adamovich in *Posledniye novosti*, 4 October 1928. Khodasevich even opined that a wonderful work of art could be produced by encoding and replaying all the drama's rhythms without any of its meanings.

32. See G.S. Smith, 'Logaoedic Metres in the Lyric Poetry of Marina Tsvetayeva', *Slavonic and East European Review*, 132, July 1975.

33. Brodsky, p. 192.

34. Vladislav Khodasevich, 'Zametki o stikhakh. Marina Tsvetaeva, "Molodets"', *Posledniye novosti*, Paris, 11 June 1925.

35. See note 23.

36. Under the title *Provodá* (Wires) i.e. telegraph wires, suggesting the similar word *próvody* (a seeing-off). These poems are translated by M. Naydan in *After Russia*: see Further Reading (i) Poetry.

37. *Letters*, p. 282.

38. *Letters*, p. 17.

39. *Letters*, p. 93.

40. *Letters*, p. 168.

41. *Letters*, p. 266.

42. *Letters*, pp. 264–66.

43. *Letters*, p. 318.

44. *Letters*, p. 267.

45. *Letters*, pp. 264, 323.

46. *Letters*, p. 380.

47. A translation of this letter by Walter Arndt can be found in *Letters 1926*, p. 267.

48. *M. Tsvetaeva. Izbrannaya proza v dvukh tomakh* [M. Tsvetaeva. Selected prose in two volumes], edited by Alexander Sumerkin, with preface by Joseph Brodsky, New York, 1979 (including 'Tvoya smert', pp. 251–67, for a translation of which, by Jamey Gambrell, see *Letters 1926*).

49. *Letters*, p. 286.

50. *Letters*, p. 349.

51. *Letters*, p. 404.

52. E.g. D.S. Mirsky (1890–1939), Mark Slonim (1894–1976) and Vladislav Khodasevich (1886–1939).

53. Irma Kudrova (see note 4), p. 10.

A.L.

Text, Publication, Performance

The Russian texts from which the translations in this book were made are those in volume three, *Poemy i dramaticheskiye proizvedeniya* (Long poems and dramatic works), of *Sobraniye sochineniy v semi tomakh* (Collected Works in Seven Volumes), edited by Anna Saakyants and Lev Mnukhin and published by Ellis Lak, Moscow, 1994. *Phaedra* occupies pages 633–86; *Novogodneye* ('New Year's Letter') pages 132–36; *Poema vozdukha* ('Poem of the Air') pages 137–45; and *Popytka komnaty* ('Attempt at a Room') pages 114–19.

Phaedra was first published in the journal *Sovremennyye zapiski*, nos 36 and 37, Paris, 1928; 'New Year's Letter' in the journal *Versty*, no. 3, Paris, 1928; 'Poem of the Air' in the journal *Volya Rossii*, no. 1, Prague, 1930; and 'Attempt at a Room' in *Volya Rossii*, no. 3, Prague, 1928.

For many years Tsvetaeva's work was not published in the Soviet Union. Then in 1961 a small book of her poems appeared, and four years later the important 'Biblioteka poeta' (Poet's Library) edition containing much of her work, though with big omissions. These books circulated rapidly but remained hard to obtain: people went straight to the black market to find them. When stage readings of her poetry began to be held, this was for a long time against the resistance of the authorities. Not until the 1980s, with the advent of the age of *glasnost'*, was Tsvetaeva fully published and no longer prohibited.

Phaedra was performed at the Taganka Theatre in Moscow in 1988 under the direction of Roman Viktyuk, with Phaedra played by the famous actress Alla Demidova. A performance took place at the Pushkin Theatre in Moscow on 8 October 2009 (for the 117th anniversary of Tsvetaeva's birth) under the French director Lukas Hemleb. In London in 1990 an adaptation of the play made by Michael Glenny and Richard Crane (apparently unpublished) was performed at the Lyric Theatre, Hammersmith. In 1991 S. Loucachevsky directed a performance of the play at the Théâtre de l'Athénée in Paris.

PHAEDRA

DRAMATIS PERSONAE

PHAEDRA
THESEUS
HIPPOLYTUS
NURSE
SERVANTS
FRIENDS OF HIPPOLYTUS (YOUNG HUNTSMEN)
SERVING-MAIDS
MESSENGER

SCENE ONE

THE HALT

Forest. Hippolytus among his friends.

CHORUS OF YOUNG HUNTSMEN, HIPPOLYTUS'S FRIENDS

O thickets! O cry!
New hills and new heights!
O mountains!
Sing praise of the chase!
What's better than fighting?
Hunting!

To Artemis praise – for the heat, the sweat,
the blackness of thickets – Hades' gates
no darker! – for pine, for foliage,
for hot hands held in the play of streams.
To Artemis praise for whatever teems
in forests.

An ambush, and fear:
Our fate, or a branch?
A branchy
bush – or a deer?
No – a sprinting shade:
Callisto!

To Artemis praise – for riverbanks, fords,
for running at chokingly breathless speed
down gorges all crammed with leafage.
As loud as the waters that race in Spring!
To Artemis praise for the joy in your heart
and sinews.

A branch in your eye.
A stump, a boar?
A scaly
coil? Root-lump?
With a wild beast's leap –
to the valley!

To Artemis praise – for keen sight and smell.
You can't blow pollen off stamens without
brushing against her. O woodland scenes!
O scent! Torrid lips in the play of a stream . . .
When you're chasing after a stag you become
a stag!

Brow flowing, mouth dry.
To your up-lifted nose –
smell of moss and fur –
horn, moss: their smell!
Like bellows – your breast.
Ho! . . . echo!

To Artemis praise – for the harm, the shame,
the joy that must fail and the track that fails.
False move, and all pains in vain!
For the supper that hid and a night in the ditch!
To Artemis praise for all our sport
in woodlands.

Catch made. Heat sleeps.
A coolness. A halt.
The hunter checks
bloodied chest and flank,
disembowels
his capture.

To Artemis praise – for the horn, the tusk,
the last of our daring, the hunter's last
shout, and the groaning forest
when turned upside down, its roots all dust!
To Artemis praise for – fur, for – flies'
buzz. Breath gone.

We don't need women!
Now and for ever
we glorify friendship,
we glorify courage!
No softness in *us*
for wives or progeny!
Let's celebrate brotherhood,
celebrate chastity!
A house and a family?
No! Forest and mystery!
We'll be called the wild ones,
the army of Artemis.
Run as the stag runs –
skimming earth's surface!
Celebrate swiftness,
celebrate breathlessness!
Don't chant that you're upright!
Tender lips can bend you!
To love is to stoop:
sing of not-loving!
Some sweetnesses lead
into boiling pitch.
Marry – and moan:
we sing of not-marrying!

Forest, green forest!
Water fast-flowing!
An archer's no settler.
Marrying means settling –
no pits and no peaks,
just gradual murder!
A proud man's no parent:
get infants – lose impetus!

Scarcely given – it's taken back!
Brief, brief – the hunter's lot.
All his flowers fade in a trice,
faster than an arrow's flight!
Waters pour, troubles heap.
The hunter's hunted by them all:

night, path, stone, dream –
everything, and everywhere
the hidden gods, who are drawn to valour,
not to cleverness of priests.
A brave man hasn't long to live:
he's himself marked out as prey.
Deity is never drawn to
high-flown projects, but to youth.
Marble's fond of sunburn: each
boy is bread-bearer to a god.
More jealous than a dancing-girl,
deity's drawn to transient things.
Far more than we need them,
the marble ones need us.

Here – the forest! Here – the bow!
None of Artemis's servants,
rugged band of troglodytes,
will ever fall in love.
Here – the age! Here – the golden!
None of Artemis's children,
distant-sighted as they are,
will ever end up married!

Now and forever,
up hills, down gullies,
sing of the goddess,
the one-only friend
of our doing and daring –
green-haired Artemis.

Loudly and fully,
in myths, in guises,
sing of the dawn-god's
twin, the majestic
any-man's-equal
wide-striding Artemis.

More lasting than watermills,
more lasting than grindstones,

ever green as the laurel,
ever free as the sea –
she in our hearts of clay is eternal:
supernal-throated Artemis.

Surviving a hundred ,
I'll crash down on one.
When the hour arrives
for the breaking of ribs,
so long as we're breathing
keep on and on singing
of friendly-to-women,
disdainful-of-men,
secretive Artemis.

Praise her more loudly!
In darkness, at daybreak
there she goes with her hound,
there she goes with her doe,
among flocks of leaves,
by night and by day,
her knee outpacing
her gown – her bracelet! – her comb! – her ribbon! –
her run runs ahead of her body.

Through haze-green mazes
she goes with her nymph,
the faithful Callisto,
never cooling
in fervour, in ardour,
her shadow not keeping up with her movement,
losing itself in the turns of her run.
Leading no-one, a leader.

Absolute happiness –
can we behold it?
She's here in the thicket,
she's here in our hearts.
Forest with motley
floor – form ranks! –

so, enclosed by a fence of stems
(trees for walls!), she'll entrust her limbs,
exhausted from running, to running water . . .

Time – surrender, and foam – disperse!
Clothing cannot catch up with knees:
sit on a stump, whatever's disgraced;
shadows cannot catch up with speed –
in despite of time, we shall go on;
breast cannot catch up with breath –
in despite of time, we'll pursue the chase;
plaits cannot catch up with nape,
nor echo with ear, nor epoch with poet . . .
But the run of the stag is caught up by the run
of Artemis.

Glorify her in leaves, in grasses!
Dense leaves – they're her curls.
Glorify her in twigs, in branches!
Branches? No – her hands and feet.
Whatever longs to break free is hers!
Each clench of strength – the muscles are hers!
Friends, honour her, even in turf!
Black roots – they are her will.
Unshakeable – her heart,
bare clods of earth – her heart!

Wild beast howling, wild woods blowing,
alone or in union
we'll sing of the lily
which never befouls
pure-white robes with the filth of love:
stone-hearted Artemis.

At the right time, slay us,
last of all arrows!
Come sing of the innocence,
praise the high pride
of the flesh that's known by none but the lake!
Quivering-nostrilled Artemis.

But a marvel – through leaves!
As if in a mist . . .
Now let us acclaim,
in song and in thought,
next to our goddess threatening-to-men:
stag-eyed Hippolytus –
mouth shut tight
against languor, mouth –
a bow, unbreakable!
Praise to our goddess's
lofty friend –
woman-resistant Hippolytus.

Nose scents the acrid,
brow shifts the bulky.
Son of King Theseus,
Grandson of Aegeus,
hater of womankind, we sing
Hippolytus of Troezen.

We'll scatter thunderclouds, shift thickets,
chanting all the while his praises,
the virginal goddess's
favourite, unsocial,
most loved of all, unsociable –
Hippolytus the uncatchable.

His hearing – a wonder, his sight – a miracle:
Flung by sleep beneath a bush,
who's most alert, who's keenest-sighted?
Hippolytus! Hippolytus!
No one has ever taken tribute
from Hippolytus the uncatchable.

Boar, take heed! Deer, shed tears!
Famous for his measuring eye –
who's most exact, most quick to seize?
Hippolytus! Hippolytus!
Lighter leaps none ever leapt
than Hippolytus the unpassable.

Scaler of bushes in hot pursuit!
And who in the daily hours of prayer,
who is most steadfast, most devout?
Hippolytus! Hippolytus! –
never putting to shame the name
of Hippolytus the unweariable.

Women rise, the sun comes out –
surrounded and entwined with women,
who is the shyest of all, the quietest?
Hippolytus! Hippolytus!
None ever slipped off with less of a glance
than Hippolytus the implacable.

Whole boar at a feast.
Sweat thirsting for grapes.
Only Hippolytus doesn't eat,
only Hippolytus doesn't drink.
Why, when he has crowned the kill,
when he's dethroned the wondrous boar –
why is he alone morose,
he alone displeased by food?
Was there a maiden in the woods?
Did the lion take doe for girl?
Or, like taking boar for fox,
is it us he takes for girls?
Fats and juices – pour and cut!
Time is dear – pour out and drink!
Woman-fighter, drink and eat!
Boar-deposer, drink and join us,
sing the praise of whirled and whirling
youth – the irretrievable!
Tipsy the grapes.
Boarmeat to grab.
How long are you young?
Remember!

HIPPOLYTUS
Boar – no joy.
Forest – no joy.

Life – no joy.
I have dreamed
a dream. Who for me transcends all women,
my mother, visited my dream.
The lady who lives only in me
came to visit her home. *This*
is the urn for her ashes! this the only
house for her anywhere on earth.
I didn't see, though the night was light,
how she entered or how she left.
When I am grey I shall say, as now,
it wasn't an entrance, it was simply:
'Here I am!' – like a boat from waves,
or something appearing out of the earth,
coming through stone, prohibition, time.
No face. Only a staring of eyes.
No stars, no rays, the stare
of her whole body, her whole soul:
like – the gaze of a doe at its fawn,
like – the gaze of mothers when they are
dead . . .
. . . Along the rims of mirrors
the gaze grew into a countenance –
circles from a thrown stone!
Bridge of the nose. In two arcs,
level brows. Beneath the lip –
stony will-power, in an arc.
A slight breathing of lips: Speak!
No speech sounded. Only a hand's
sign. Silence's utter thunder.
Then the steady rise of a waxen
hand. An opening in the shroud.
A finger showing her son a wound.
Something melted, something floated.
Dear friends, what does it mean,
to see the breast and the wound at once?!
Nothing was said. Blood flowed
to the ground, on my hands – I lay prostrate,
helpless, while her finger floated
hovering up and up until

it came to a stop and sealed her mouth –
against her maternal words? Or mine?
Nothing else happened. There was smoke
there . . . Within ten fingers' span –
no flesh. There was a shroud,
steam! I grasp it! Mere steam. Empty.
Steam melting beneath my hand,
which is hoping . . .

ONE OF THE FRIENDS

A dream!

HIPPOLYTUS

. . . knowing . . .

FRIENDS

(speaking one after the other)

Delirium!
– Fantasy-mad!
– Crazed by a thought!
– Magic – so what?
– Fairy-tale stuff!
– Nothing but steam!
– Nothing but smoke!
– Mind-smoke!
– We are what's real.
– Everything else –
phantoms and spells.
– Eye of the full
moon, its darts'
bane. – Dear friend!
It's something you ate!
– Something you drank
too much of at night!
– When we relax
Bacchus goes wild.
– Not even moon-steam –
steams of wine.
– Brain-turning fumes!

– Dead mortals sleep!
Live mortals drink!

(together)

Spite these ravings, spite these spells –
drink and laugh, before we go bald!

A SERVANT
Mothers don't come to us from the grave
without good reason: beware, my lord.

(Phaedra enters)

PHAEDRA
Noble marksmen, I give you greetings.
Here in this wilderness of thickets,
going from herb to herb, absorbed,
I have lost all my serving-maids.
Now I can't find the right path back.
Kindly show me the way, the slope
down from this perfidious wood.
Where is the path to Troezen town?
Help me and you won't regret it.

HIPPOLYTUS
Very noble lady!
In this place of dizzying heights and terrors
nothing serves but *power* and *daring*.
(Can such belong to women?) I will offer
good advice: just stay at home in future
with your distaff, not among the briers.
But here's a guide down unsteady paths
that murder female feet.

(to another servant)

You know
the way, be the lady's guide.

PHAEDRA
Permit me
to ask what you do in this lowly world?
For there is royalty in your face.

HIPPOLYTUS

Artemis I serve. And you?
By your speech, you're a foreigner.

PHAEDRA

Aphrodite I serve. I am from Crete.

THE QUESTIONING

Phaedra, ill, among her serving-maids.

ONE OF THE MAIDS
I can hear her nurse's step.

NURSE *(entering)*
Sleeping?

SERVING-MAIDS *(speaking one after the other)*
        – Seems to be unconscious.
  – Foreign sickness. – Unknown fever.
  – Wasn't sleeping. – Nor waking either.
  – When she speaks it sounds like nonsense.
  – 'Give me something hot. No, cold.'
  – Offer a cool drink: 'Need a hot one.'
  – Steam, she turns her head away.
  – Same with clothing. – How she wearies us!
 –This way – 'freezing', that way – 'suffocating'.
  – Pull them on her, tear them off her.
  – Sees the lamp: 'Our house is burning!'
  – Cover it: 'I'm down a well-shaft!'
  – Light: her eyes hurt. Dark: she's frightened.
  – Oh such eyes, you can't describe them.
  – More than her hands, her eyes I pity.
  – How she wrings her hands and twists them.
  – More than her eyes, her hands I pity.
  – Tries to break them, tries to crush them!
  – Whisper: she'll ask you: 'Am I dying?'
  – Speak more loudly: blocks her ears up.
  – Not herself, she's not her real self.
  – Talks of forest lairs and horses.
  – Raving.

NURSE
> Know the illness – know
the balm. No asking means no cure.
Roots I've brought and special herbs.
Scoured three hills in search of them.

MAIDS *(one after the other)*
> – Says she needs a fast, fast horse.
> – Heat keeps blazing from her face.
> – Rips the bracelets from her arms.

PHAEDRA
> I hear, I hear the galloping horse!

NURSE
> That's the knocking of her heart.
> . . .
> Sleep, my milky one, sleep, my everything!
> Yet she sailed from Athens merrily,
> urged the sailors onward, onward
> with her praises, with her ecstasies
> (nearly had to bail out water),
> spied the forest: – 'Ah, those thickets!' –
> goatish jumps and hareish leaping!
> Through the undergrowth, pursuing her,
> you, all breathless, you were stumbling.
> Changed she came back from the forest.

PHAEDRA
> Lofty grows the myrtle's
> leafy bough, I tell you.
> I hear, I hear the galloping horse!

NURSE
> That's the knocking of her heart.
> . . .
> I would ask, if I were bolder,
> *what* in those dense woods she came across?
> Did she meet with wicked folk there?
> Yet her necklace isn't broken.
> Or some great-clawed forest animal?
> Then her dress would be in tatters.

Nothing (a ring – we would have found it!)
did she leave in woods' obscurity.
Only her bright cheeks. Only her soul.

MAIDS *(one after the other)*
– Listened far too long to the forest's
whispers, whispering something to her.
– I believe she ate some berries
not prescribed by our physicians.
– I believe she sniffed some blossoms
no one knows of, fever-giving.
– I believe she's pining for the
king's kisses.

PHAEDRA
                    There's a hammer
in my temples! Boiling water
running scalding down my face!
Cool the boiling!
Stop the hammer!

MAIDS
– Still she's tossing, turning, suffering!
– No amount of clever tailoring
can make a shirt to alter destiny.
– High time for the kingly homecoming.
– All her soul is hurting everywhere.
– Crying out for the king, calling him.
– Gods are merciful – he'll be coming
over the sea.

PHAEDRA
                    No, from the forest.
Nearer, nearer, the galloping horse!
Lower, lower, the dreadful bough!
Crack, skin! Flow, juice!

NURSE
Bewitched is the heart that thumps in you.
In your own breast, poor dear, is your galloping
horse. Oh, unlucky that hour we
sailed from Athens! Unlucky the hour we

reached Troezen with its three calamities.
Even incense can't move alien
gods. Why did we need to visit
foreign faces, leaving familiar ones?
What had we in Troezen? He should have
summoned his son for a long stay in Athens.
Here three sorrows – there just a half-sorrow.
True, there too there's a lot of pigeon milk.
But there the gods are our native gods.

PHAEDRA

In the woods, a lofty bough.
On the bough is heavy fruit.
The fruit sways, the bough bends.

NURSE

That's the bewitched heart beating in her.

MAIDS

Foreign fever.

NURSE

           Forest fever:
bough and horse – they're in her mind.
Fears the branch will crack. What fruit?
Fruit of her thought. What horse? There's none.

PHAEDRA

Full-gallop you'll go flying past.
Down to you I shall lean from the bough.
Heavy is the fruit to that bough.
Heavy that bough's fruit: my yearning.

NURSE

In her own brain is the splinter:
bough . . . battle of blood and reason,
one half fights the other half,
bole at war with ailing heartwood.
Ancient song, an ancient story.

MAIDS

– Shouldn't we inform the stepson?
– He's too severe.

– His heart is miserly.

PHAEDRA

The galloping's stopped!
The bough has cracked!

. . .

What is all this I see around me?
Where am I? Who am I? What am I?
Why does everything seem spellbound?
Where do I belong? Who am I?
Why is my hair all bare and floating?

NURSE

You couldn't sleep, it came undone.

PHAEDRA

Why am I half-dressed, half-undressed?

NURSE

You're no hunchback – why be shamefaced?

PHAEDRA

Sisters dear, you look so worried!

MAIDS

– All night long we trembled for you.
– Oh lady, how we feared for your life.
– All the night long, oh how I trembled . . .

PHAEDRA

Fever is talkative.
Did I say something?

NURSE

Just a mort of silly nonsense.

PHAEDRA

Did I utter someone's name?

(to the maids)

Since when are magpies stricken dumb?

MAIDS

– You did speak but we know nothing.
– Dark your thoughts and dark your cavern.

– You said a name, we can't know whose.
– Water flows – but try to weigh it!
– Who was, what was, there's no knowing . . .
– This is a new disease . . .

NURSE
                              An old one.
Older than us by far. *Our* lives
are two days long. Kings' lives are changeless.
Earlier than life it starts, the ancestral
woe – it's not a woe of orphans –
humankind itself would vanish
in an hour, be gone completely,
nor would it have ever started,
had a certain power not hurtled
down from above.

                    (to the maids)

                              But you girls don't
need to know this yet. Go, frolic
while you're foolish. I shall go and
lull my queen with lullabies,
calming, chanting –
a seabed sea-shell.
Shall I, child?

PHAEDRA
                    You shall, dear nanny.

                    (The maids go off)

NURSE
I'll tell of the faraway long-ago:
hapless women of your family's line –
this will be said of you in the future!
Pasiphaë desired a monster,
turned from the king, loved a wild beast.
Are you her daughter, or are you not?
Bad, the blood of your dear mother!
Sleeping, Ariadne was sold
to a god by one who's now your husband.
You're her sister twice:

first by womb, then by marriage-bed.
With the god she was not contented,
turned from the god, to love the dust.
There the passion, here the fear.

PHAEDRA

Difficult for me to equal
my sister, equal of a god.

NURSE

Children of the selfsame mother,
married to the selfsame husband –
luckless Pasiphaën daughters.
Ariadne – your age then –
how old would she be today?
Let us see – how old's the king?
If the god hadn't set her in heaven . . .

PHAEDRA

More than forty.

NURSE

        Yes, a lot more.
More like getting on for fifty.
That king of yours . . . he looks so old! –
now no gilding please, no buttering:
are you happy with him, Phaedra?

PHAEDRA

A shepherd can live without the sheep,
what are the sheep without the shepherd?

NURSE

Phaedra, he could be your father!
Stepfather-husband, he called himself!

PHAEDRA

Oaks grow stronger without the ivy:
that means death to the ivy stem.

NURSE

Phaedra – you don't love him!

PHAEDRA

Nanny – I do love him.

NURSE

All that suckling and all that feeding you:
pretty darling, little godsend –
then she goes and loves a greybeard . . .
how can ears take in such madness!

PHAEDRA

Is he my husband, or not?

NURSE

My aching bones, may they fall to pieces!
Yes, fair lady, but not yours only.
Count them: Ariadne's first,
then Antiope's,
Phaedra's husband today, and tomorrow?
All my feeding! Pasiphaë's
black and unrepentant blood is
turned to water! *Your* husband?
No, he's an inherited husband.
Where's the joy in that? – all right if it's
having joy in your sister's *husband,*
but, Phaedra, he's your sister's widower!
One and all will say –
the goddess's inconsolable widower!
To this day he's Ariadne's.
Ask the lord of dreams: yes,
still a widower.
Wouldn't have left you alone in the forest
here among columbines, if he'd needed you.
Phaedra, he's no husband for you.

PHAEDRA

Nanny, I am his wife.
So stop this silly talk of yours!

NURSE

Charming the way you say 'I love him' –
Even a serving-girl guards the hearth.
What is 'I love'? No, no, it's *how*

you love! After ten years of marriage
things grow clear – how, why, for what
you love him. Well then?

PHAEDRA

First – he is brave.

NURSE

All birds have wings, all fish have gills,
everywhere the men are brave.
What else?

PHAEDRA

He speaks in a friendly way
to passers-by.

NURSE

He talks a lot?
Who to, though? That's your second reason.
Third?

PHAEDRA

He's generous . . .

NURSE

So – a treasure!
Brave and kind, you say – and then –
similar sort of thing again!
Almost nothing new in it.
What else? –

PHAEDRA

He honours distant kin.
And I've plenty to tell of the wherefore and why!

NURSE

Grind more finely. Strength, simplicity –
these have nothing to do with loving.
What more?

PHAEDRA

Theseus's grey hairs –
aren't they signs of wisdom?

NURSE

                  Sow
more thickly, I tell you – your sieve is rubbish!
Wise! What else?

PHAEDRA

               He deals with the conquered
kindly.

NURSE

      That all?

PHAEDRA

              Very simply –
he is my husband.

NURSE

            That's a fine word
squeezed from your mouth. And nothing more?
Nightingales are glad to trill of
everything in the garden. No more to it?
Let me speak, then. Why I attack
Theseus: he's too old.
Phaedra, they mated you with a spider!
Take revenge on him, give up make-believe,
you're not guilty in any way.
Into your husband's house
you came, a late-coming wife, the third of them.
Two wives met with the new young wife at the
threshold, two wives not of this earth
led the young one in.
'Here', they said to her, 'live, enjoy yourself',
took the younger wife's hands and guided her.
Phaedra, all of your nights and days
pass beneath their shade.
If your bed is dark, that's the cloud they cast on it.
Two wives whisper to you interferingly.
Plates fly suddenly out of your hands?
That's the Amazon's keen
glance – don't go looking behind the drapery!
Everywhere, house and courtyard, everything
stares with their eyes. If your hearth goes cold

that's Ariadne's breath.
Their heart is fierce and their place is sanctified.
Young wife, matched with the Styx by two other wives.
Lift a cup to your lips to drink –
that's Ariadne's iron
ladle. Handing out berries, grapes? They are
Ariadne's tears and Antiope's.
Set down the cup from your mouth –
that's the Amazon's sour
taste and also the taste of Theseus's
mouth – *embittered* by what she did to him?
If your night-lamp oil runs dry –
that's Ariadne's sign,
secret. The walls are stifling, mouldering.
Two wives cursed the young wife's fertility.
When you get up you're just the same
as when you lay down:
scant wife, wife all empty, minimal.
Two serpents' eyes are fixed on the marital
couch. No laughter is heard in the house.
There's Ariadne's sob
for a child. A soul's sob would be kindlier.
Two wives? No – two serpents. If to this
day, Phaedra, your belt's not tight
that's the Amazon's work.
What miry shore, what verge of marshiness,
you have settled on! Bed bewitched by the
chilling patterns and shapes of *their*
shoulders and thighs.
Don't hide your face in your hands! I'm telling you –
marriage without a child is lechery.

PHAEDRA
   With a child I'd rejoice. Without,
   I'm not grieving.

NURSE
               Who gives no joy
  doesn't deserve either joy or children.
  'In love shall you multiply' – that's the law
  for all your kind, that's how it is.

Mother revere father –
not enough for a fine generation!
A useless wife, a wife all emptiness . . .

PHAEDRA
I've listened to you! Now please . . .

NURSE
                                    You're right!
I must listen now.
Like someone stolen, you love your husband.
Why then are your cheeks so hollow?

PHAEDRA
It's because . . .

NURSE
                    You're lying!
To me, to yourself, to him, to others.
I have suckled you with my breast –
you and I don't need to use words:
I know, I sense, I see, I hear
everything, all your buried griefs!
This means I know five times more
than you know, sense, and see, and wish
to know. . .

PHAEDRA
                    Old woman, you nag like doubt.

NURSE
. . . wish, thirst, dare to know, and can.

PHAEDRA
Old woman, you gnaw at living flesh.

NURSE
I'm weary of waiting.
Say it! Out with it!
I'm still the wetnurse,
you're still the fosterling.
How hard a word's first syllable!
Between my bosom and your mouth,
between these poor, generous nipples

and your lips, no room for secrets.
Where could they be, between mouth and breast,
two fully nourished passions.
Trembling is the nurse's breast.
Secrets, sorrows, troubles – cast them
off your shoulders! Onto my heart!
All your sadnesses at once!
This breast can't be overloaded.
Now, no roundabout phrases, lavish
oaths. I am still wetnurse, you are
still the fosterling! – See, I am
mother to you, and you my daughter.
There is a voice besides the voice of
blood: the voice of milk – let's yield to
milk. A second motherhood.
Two destinies govern human lives:
voice of blood and voice of milk.
Motherhood gushes from the heart,
daughterhood's in the sucking lips.
Should a poison flow in the veins,
I must answer, I'm the nourisher.
This bond is strong as the grave.
Where are those days now?
I'm still wetnurse. You're still fosterling.
Night is poor in all but thought.
Feed upon my wisdom, just as
once you fed (so sweet those hours!)
upon my milk, and it was whiter
than goddess-foam. Upon my youth!
Cloth you weave I alone can see.

PHAEDRA
Old woman, how you prattle on.

NURSE
Your dreams, are they ever dreamed in families?

PHAEDRA
Old woman, you are sowing slanders.

NURSE
Lovely girl, surely

it's *my* sins you sin?
All of them – nurse-dreams!
You're the fosterling
only. Ask
a surgeon dealing with an ulcer:
he cuts cleanly, he cuts quickly.
Ask the headsman at the scaffold:
he cleaves cleanly, cleaves at a stroke.
Queen, it's not the king you're fond of!

PHAEDRA

Nurse, you cut into living flesh.

NURSE

Queen – it's not the king you love!

PHAEDRA

Nurse, you cleave through living flesh.
I implore you by all my torments:
when will they end?

NURSE

             Phaedra, the name!
All this asking
has drained my prayers.
I'm no wetnurse,
you're no fosterling,
So, my milk was all wasted, splashed on the
ground! Or is he of such low birth, to
name him is harder than lifting a ton?

PHAEDRA

He – of low birth? Oh no. Lofty –
loftiest of all.

NURSE

           Hm. With bedsores?
Men go to war and he lies with his wife,
belt undone, like any drunkard?

PHAEDRA

Too young to wed, too brave to be idle.
When war-trumpets sound he'll be the first

to rush to the fray.

NURSE

No coward, you say – that indeed would be shameful,
no slave, you say – no bull from the slaughter
drying your mind up . . . some sort of god, then?
Whoever it is, it is not too dreadful –
unless it's your own son.

PHAEDRA

My stepson.
Son of kings. The end. No secret.
Only do not pronounce his name.
I shall not endure the sound!

NURSE

I won't pronounce a letter of it.
Why, my dear, why did you hide
from this the loyallest of nurses?
Marvellous, marvellous is our bond.

PHAEDRA

I am hiding from myself.

NURSE

Gods will envy him: is it long
since you confessed your love to him?

PHAEDRA

When they come with the flaming torch,
along with Phaedra they will burn
her secret.

NURSE

Hide your face with your hand!

PHAEDRA

Shame beyond the reach of thought!
If from words alone my brow
turns blood-red . . .

NURSE

What could be simpler?
Choose an hour that hides it all –

the brow, the shame upon it . . . choose
thickest thickets. Night and bushes,
they're well used to hiding . . .

PHAEDRA

                              Me?
With him? In the woods?

NURSE

                    Take the nearest path.

PHAEDRA

A path I'm not able to see!
A step into rings of black.
One step – and fall as dead . . .

NURSE

Be able! The quietest hour.

PHAEDRA

This is a sound I cannot hear.
This is a sound unthinkable
from pure lips . . .

NURSE

              You love – and pure
feelings are rare. The quietest hour . . .

PHAEDRA

Ravings. Heart, you mustn't listen!

NURSE

. . . hour that's seen so much and knows
for us, the latest hour of all,
our hour! The only hour of the day
that tells no lies. And choose the densest
bush, the sleepiest slope . . .

PHAEDRA

                      The grass,
the leaves – they won't endure it!

NURSE

                    You're
unused to such matters! Straighten up!

Aren't you in love with this boy? . . . Now take
the very deepest breath you can,
the fullest ladleful of breath.

PHAEDRA

But I cannot breathe at all!
No strength! No hands! No feet! No sinews!
My mouth won't speak! My chest will burst!
One syllable and I'm in Hell!
No such words exist!

NURSE

There's one,
simplest of all, and everything's in it.

PHAEDRA

So, do you want me worse than dead –
despicable?

NURSE

In the myrtle bushes –
lips to lips! – Today! At once!
Phaedra!

PHAEDRA

Witch!

NURSE

Phaedra!

PHAEDRA

Bawd!
Ah – set – me – free!

NURSE

I'm the one who brought you up!

PHAEDRA

I was proud and pure.

NURSE

I'm the one who suffered for you!

PHAEDRA

This – shame – I can't accept.

NURSE

We will hide it, bury it, trample it,
bury and hide and trample the shame!

PHAEDRA

A tree will make a sound, give warning.

NURSE

Tear and trim and tie the leaves.

PHAEDRA

Nurse! But he's a woman-hater.
The very sight of hair that reaches
down to the shoulders . . .

NURSE

. . . the thicker he'll plait it,
loose the plaits and weave them up.

PHAEDRA

He'll never untie himself from his brethren,
his comrades in work, their youthful feasting.

NURSE

Give *them* the day, *we*'ll have the night.
We shall not offend the marksmen.

PHAEDRA

But – with or without them – he's
a worshipper of Artemis.

NURSE

All the higher will be the honour –
conquered in no simple battle!

PHAEDRA

But, far more than any other –
he's an abuser of Aphrodite . . .

NURSE

All the greater, then, the gain.
Who hasn't slept can't be awakened.

PHAEDRA

But – I am his elder by ten years!

Waves of the river can't flow backward.

NURSE

All the more purely will he burn!
Your ten years will be like straw!

PHAEDRA

I'm as a mother to him, the people
call him my son . . .

NURSE

                    Honouring both
the passion and the mother in you,
all the more softly will he spread
his couch – you'll steer it like a boat.

PHAEDRA

I am married! I'm a wife!
My husband . . .

NURSE

                    Don't say *my*, say *our*
husband! You'll be paying him back
for your sister's grief, that dreadful splash of
cowardly oars . . .

PHAEDRA

                    But the king's not only
my husband – he is his father.

NURSE

                            Ashamed
to cling? The link will be the stronger,
loyalty the sturdier.

PHAEDRA

If he rejects me?

NURSE

                    Who – the king?

PHAEDRA

The *king*?

NURSE

Who then?

PHAEDRA

He who . . .

NURSE

He

reject *you*?! All my blood shudders!
Not important you're a beauty:
anyone lovely – always someone
lovelier. The goddess took
all the beauty, then bade us share it.
Not important you're a queen. His
shoulders' breadth is what allured you,
not the noble line he comes from.
Nor does your intelligence matter . . .
After every clever word
there's a doubly clever one.
To all extremes – power, reason, sweetness –
a greater reason, sweetness, power.
To power, your being a queen is nothing.
As for reason . . . You in your right mind?
No, all lovers I've ever met were
out of their minds!

PHAEDRA

So what good thing
is left in me?

NURSE

The magic charm
of Aphrodite. He'll give up
utterly – count them, one by one:
as woman-hater – his childish pride;
huntsman – he'll renounce the hunt,
that challenge to his birth and kin;
as son and friend and worshipper –
abandon his sacrificial slabs
and Artemis, his whole soul,
for the sake of Aphrodite!
For a slave of Aphrodite!

So, go on, just simply love him,
love your beardless marksman. See, I'm
feeding on your youth, as once –
sweet hours! – you used to feed on mine.
Then, so the milk should not run dry,
I ate and drank for two. And now,
you – sin for two, caress for two,
have joy and pain.
Almost – utmost –
all to – all your
soul to – me. No
board with strings can sound as finely
as a loving breast. Your hand!
You love him?

PHAEDRA

        Hush!

NURSE

              For what?

PHAEDRA

                        Closer . . .

NURSE

For his speech?

PHAEDRA

              But do I hear it?

NURSE

For his looks?

PHAEDRA

              But do I see him?
Sultry eyelids. My name means 'shining'.

NURSE

For his chasteness?

PHAEDRA

              Am I worthy?

NURSE

For his heart?

PHAEDRA

          But do I know it?
If I knew it – into the pit!
If I knew it – into the earth!
I love him for everything,
everything, everything,
I love him for *this* life,
the present, the future . . .

NURSE

What else?

PHAEDRA

       Nothing else.

NURSE

So, you love him.
Well, to please your
youthful marksman,
how will you dress?

PHAEDRA

I haven't thought.

NURSE

Madness at night
mustn't betray you.

PHAEDRA

Haven't thought of
any *afterwards*.
Love is an unknown
land, a forest.

NURSE

Your beloved is here, the king is abroad,
the hour is precious: use it well.
You are timid. You must make
everything very smooth for him.

PHAEDRA

I fear you're whispering
things that are wrong.
In untried hands

even kingdoms crumble . . .

NURSE

Whisper into his ear!

PHAEDRA

I haven't the courage
even for whispering!
I'll stare at the ground,
one word – and I'll die . . .

NURSE

Write him a letter –
what's writing for
if not for letters?
We're not teaching birds
how to eat berries,
they know all that!
I'll give the letter,
you'll give the lips.

PHAEDRA

No oars, no shores!
All adrift at once!

NURSE

Upon a cliff
there grew a tall tree.

PHAEDRA

Trust . . . ? Put faith . . .?

NURSE

Laurel-walnut-almond!
Upon a goodly tree
no shame to hang yourself!

SCENE THREE

THE CONFESSION

Hippolytus's lair. Hippolytus and an aged servant.

SERVANT
  Arrow hissing. Blood spurting.
  All I can say.

HIPPOLYTUS
            So tell me again,
  tell me it all.

SERVANT
            Ranks surrounded her.
  Arrow – out. Blood gushing . . .
  And a son had lost his mother.
  That is all there is to tell you,
  no more of Antiope for you,
  green tree that she was, inflexible,
  Theseus's sombre wife, Hippolytus's
  luckless mother. Breath – to the world,
  beauty – to dust, sight – into light.
  All I can tell you. Nothing more
  of her red lips.
            I've had my fill
  of living, longing. But still I see,
  through a cloud of twice-seven years,
  how she fought beside your father,
  Amazon against her tribe,
  flesh fighting kindred flesh,
  daughter of man-hating hordes,
  herself against herself! Ring-finger's
  quarrel with the middle finger.
  First and last time (middle finger's
  fight with palm!) in all three years

spent in that vale of women, that
fierce-fleshed throng, the daughter
clad herself in martial armour,
dazzling every eye that saw her.
And each one's breast was cleft for war,
and a sigh was sighed of more than love,
a single sigh through both the camps.
What a furnace! What a battle!
To this very day, I tell you,
icy shivers go down my spine:
how she fought beside your father,
tightening – surely her own sinew,
sinew of woman's will! – her bowstring:
wondrous the upsurging bow that seemed,
to gods and humans both, a doubled
female breast, outlined in air,
a wave beating against a galley!
Taking aim, not just with eye and
elbow, but with every pulsing
vein, aiming her whole aimed
body, equal of men – no, equal
of gods (her never-used-up quiver
fuller than a horn of plenty),
radiant under the foe's arrows,
there she stood, afraid of nothing.
Bowstring taunting tauter bowstrings,
fleshless bosom turned aside and
merging with the chest-tight bow so
close the arrows seemed to fly
not from the string but from the heart! Those
arrows passionate for destruction,
so thick and fast, in endless sequence,
that they could have been (but was it
war or thread she span?) a single
arrow flying from the string.
Was that a lion fighting beside her?
No, for in that cruel battle
even a god would have seemed timid.
Facing arrows, spurning pleasures,
thus she fought beside your father.

HIPPOLYTUS
Fought for him?

SERVANT
No, for her son.
Fought, the brood-hen, for her fledgling,
fought for her son's inheritance. And
died for him – so fine a woman –
for her son's supremacy.
All for her son – against her kin –
she fell, that Athens might be his:
pure sacrifice of motherhood.

HIPPOLYTUS
I shall die childless. Not for the first time
do I grieve for that. I'll neither
prolong the noble line of Theseus
with deeds of a prolific race
nor pass on to my sons a queen's
sinews, a queen's strength.
In vain the sinew, in vain the strength.
From me no cradle: I am a tomb for
both my mother and my father.
Let me tell the heaviest sorrow
last. Not the land but the honeycombs
gained by me through my mother's blood
and father's sweat: into the hands of
whose son shall I pass them on?
Fatherless, spit upon the childless!
Wandering rogue, you beget your like.
From the most ridden of jades – a god!
From riding none – a rolling stone!

SERVANT
That's an ancient tune. Even
a baby in a fit of fretting
will refuse the breast, but once he
firmly takes it, who'll drag him off?!
More drunk than a baby, you'll start to suckle –
you're not the first to call it trash!
Everyone slandered it – you will praise it,

today resisting, tomorrow yielding.
Everyone spat on it – you will swallow it
infinitely . . . On a tender bosom
all is put right!

HIPPOLYTUS

No hope of that!
I hate those hair-in-ringlets serpents
just as Antiope hated men!
All of them stranglers, all of them cats
playing with mice!

SERVANT

Well, who are you
yourself if not a son of woman?

HIPPOLYTUS

Look up at the sky! Of an eagle, not
a fat-rumped woman. Don't you see?
Hatred of woman – converse side of
hatred of man: the family's finished! –
I drank it in with my mother's milk.

NURSE *(entering)*

Just so, clever man (and cripple).
Monk or reveller – all come from milk,
all from the white . . . Do *they* govern?
No, it's milk that governs the world.
The whole world's ruled by milk alone!
And next, my lord, a little matter
just for your ears – a mouse in a crack –
only your ears, I say, and no one
else's. Two won't be enough,
you ought to have been born with five.
My message isn't for aged granddads.

(The servant goes out)

Lean your fine ear to me, my lord.
Here's a berry, ripe for picking . . .

(Hands Hippolytus a letter and goes out)

HIPPOLYTUS

'To Theseus's son Hippolytus, in secret.'
That word's repulsive to my ears.
Secret? Zeus's temple is built
openly. If it isn't poisoned,
food's cooked openly. Even treasure,
after it has lain a while,
rings out loudly from underfoot.
Innocence seeks the light of day.
– A huntsman won't be caught in a trap! –
Openly wedding couches are spread.
Enemies, if not wholly evil,
take aim openly. Except for monsters
all live openly. Except for lechery,
all's done openly. Shunned by the sun,
the blind man shows his blank eye to all,
the deaf-mute moos his grief to all.
Bowels of the earth show in roots, and roots
openly show in the tree as a whole.
'Thicket, hide' . . . thus innocent blood
speaks the truth through bushes.
                                        See!
No matter what this letter holds,
writer, your labour was in vain!
No reader of a secret letter
is Hippolytus. And I smash
more than the tablet! With this wax
I smash – like wax – intrigues, seditions,
every slander, secret, snare,
all that steams and isn't water,
all that bakes and doesn't smoke,
all that whispers – lips behind a
grating – won't speak out loud and clear,
everything sticky, slippery, creeping:
secret, here is your exposure!

            (*Throws down the tablet*)

Those who know not, let them hear!
Thus Hippolytus writes his answers.

(Phaedra appears, her finger to her lips)

PHAEDRA
Shsh . . .

HIPPOLYTUS
   What's this? . . . Am I delirious?
There's a woman in my quarters!
Her feet are bare, her braids dishevelled . . .
Who are you? Do you come to die
or to sell? Go, ask a higher price –
you've made a mistake, it's the wrong bed!
This is no chamber – it's a lair!

PHAEDRA
Just two words, two syllables!

HIPPOLYTUS
No syrup-seller – it's an ambush!

PHAEDRA
For half a glance, for half a murmur,
mite of a murmur, trace of an echo . . .
blink of an eyelid, an eye's glance!
In the name of the Goddess of Foam,
look at me: am I not known to you
in any feature, is it all so
new, does nothing of me tell you . . .
have my eyes, then . . .

HIPPOLYTUS
      You disturb me,
shadow!

PHAEDRA
   . . . lost so terribly their
brightness? Oh, of course – I knew it! –
when you looked at me so slightly,
so inscrutably, so blindly . . .
looked, not *at* me – looked – past me!
All that beauty of mine! As if a
sponge had absorbed it, yet my features,
lips: grief hadn't twisted them.

Look at me! Is this the first time you have
seen me?

HIPPOLYTUS
                    On my oath! All – vanished!

PHAEDRA
    Out of an island known as Crete
    did not your widowed father bring me . . .

HIPPOLYTUS
    My stepmother! Wife of the king!
    What delusion! Gross delirium!
    How could I, of all men, so
    injure – insult – the wife of Theseus?
    So forget her!

PHAEDRA
                    So not see her,
    not see at all, though close beside you!

HIPPOLYTUS
    The hour so late, your changed appearance . . .
    hair unfastened, and no headband . . .
    unaccustomed . . .

PHAEDRA
                    My prompting helps –
    you've recognised me!

HIPPOLYTUS
                    How put right
    my wrong? And yet, at such an hour
    when even the guards . . . There must be some
    especial need for you to enter
    Hippolytus's lair with ghostly
    step, the look of someone . . .

PHAEDRA
                                drunken!

HIPPOLYTUS
    What brings you here?

PHAEDRA

A mortal wound.
If you repent of having spoken
thoughtlessly, now swear, by all I'm
breaking with, give me your word
you'll hear me out, not interrupt.

HIPPOLYTUS
Word of a son!

PHAEDRA

No, better say:
word of a man!

HIPPOLYTUS

Not of a woman!

PHAEDRA
Don't destroy the olive-twig.
Word of a man!

HIPPOLYTUS

Of an Amazon's son.

PHAEDRA
You above us – do you hear this?

HIPPOLYTUS
Queen, *I* heard. I'm listening to you.
Courteously, quietly.

PHAEDRA

The beginning
was – a glance. A footstep. Paths with
no way down. I've got it wrong, there
was a bush, a myrtle bush. I've
lost my way, I'm like a schoolboy
muddling letters! – the beginning
was a horn's sound – sound of thickets –
turning into a sound of goblets!
But what's the sound of ringing brass
next to a sound that came from unseen
lips! A bush. A crunch. Pulling
the bush apart . . . I'm getting

lost, I'm like a sluttish drunkard.
In the beginning was a knocking
heart – *before* the bush, *before*
the horn, before it all – a knocking,
just as though I'd met a god – a
knocking, just as though I'd moved a
boulder! The beginning was
you, in sounds of horn and brass
and rustling forest . . .

HIPPOLYTUS

Either you're raving –

PHAEDRA

. . . you through branches, you through eyelids,
you through killed things . . .

HIPPOLYTUS

– or *I* am mad.

PHAEDRA

The deathly isn't written – whispered.

HIPPOLYTUS

Can I be hearing this?

PHAEDRA

For you
I was brought up in the wilds of Crete.

HIPPOLYTUS

Do you speak of . . . that? Of . . . you?

PHAEDRA

Unassailable – for others!
That, my dearest. *I*, my dearest!
Carried pearl-quiet in the heart's
valves . . .

HIPPOLYTUS

O that I hadn't sworn . . . !

PHAEDRA

. . . in the womb's secret depths more sweetly
than a firstborn . . .

HIPPOLYTUS

Oh that I hadn't

sworn as a son!

PHAEDRA

I am dead, and therefore

know no shame! Those stars!

HIPPOLYTUS

Those chasms!

PHAEDRA

My little tree! My lofty cliff!
Oh, those curls!

HIPPOLYTUS

Those ghastly locks!

PHAEDRA

Help me understand, I'm stupid!
Even jealous of the elk-skins
strewn for carpets in this cave.
Once there was a little tree –
gave its plenteous shade to travellers.
It was I who burned it down
with my frenzy, with my yearning.
Each sigh cost the poor tree a leaf –
how red it was, you can't conceive!
As many leaves as there were sighs,
each new leaf – its life dried out.
As many sighs as there were leaves,
as many sobs and smotherings . . .
Shining? No, oh no, the shadow
of a shadow! All the colour –
on Hippolytus's bed. You took
no aim, but hit the mark. A small
child would laugh: no shot, but a kill.
Yet beneath a marriage coverlet
sleep with you would be too little.
Night is short – we'd rise and shiver.
What's a sleep if in the morning
we must wake to common daylight?

No, I'm dreaming of a different
sleep – of one we'll never wake from –
the bed is spread for us already –
not a night's sleep – sleep eternal,
never-ending . . . let them weep! –
where no stepsons are, no stepmothers,
where no sins live on in children,
no grey-bearded husbands, no third
wives . . .
Just once! I'm all burnt up from waiting!
While we have arms, while we have lips!
It will be glimpsed – it won't be spoken of!
One word, say one word to me! . . .

HIPPOLYTUS

Reptile!

THE LITTLE TREE

NURSE *(over Phaedra's body)*
Where is she sleeping?
She's not in her bed.
Whispers float down:
the myrtle has borne
an unknown fruit –
eyes – what juice!
teeth – what fruit!
Breezes began
blowing – the fruit
swung to and fro,
swung back and forth
again and again –
who will dare pluck
this fruit from the tree?
Desired by the flies,
shunned by the bees.
Wonder unheard-of:
the myrtle has flowered
with flesh! A sight
unheard-of! More green
than fruit, a queen
hangs, and the birds
fly round her. Away
from her wide-open eyes!
Shoo, kites, begone!
I shan't let you feed
on her agate eyes!
Oh the horn doesn't sound
and the clang of the storm
is silent. I kept
thinking: this once –

from him only – some
goodness will come,
but see – in her girdle
she hangs! in her hair –
bird in a snare,
fish in a net.
'Cut her down!
I've waited all night
for the gardener, but where's
a gardener for this
fruit?' The old one's
fled, and the young
holds up his horn,
jumps over a ditch,
doesn't think to look
at his wonderful catch –
let it wait – I've no time!
The fruit scarcely holds,
the branch scarcely holds.
Woman-slanderer,
skinflint and thief!
Who flew from red lips,
who froze and went numb
when he met brown eyes?
– Bushes, don't tell!
Loving has failed
but her honour we'll save!

Myrtle bush, screen her
from tree-stump and bee!
I'll whiten you
with the blackness of *him*.
You'll be for the king
what you've always been.
I'll blacken that man
with the blackness of you.

Those whom the gods mean to destroy,
first – alas! – they make insane.
She – the untouchable – to love

such a blind and stupid fool!
Rather than be alone with his queen
he takes his dog and roams the woods!
Wind, whistle! Branches, crack!

. . . Such a savage, clumsy fool!
Animals are skinned more kindly
than he spoke to her dear soul.
Gentle love, my lady queen –
you loved a heartless flayer of beasts.
Which of us – am I asleep? –
which is the sleeper, of us two?
Noose around your neck for so
stupid a stepson? Worse – a whelp.
Notch this on a branch, you dark
forests – such a merry joke! –
how the queen, for a vile cur,
hanged herself upon a tree!
And how I myself – but *how*? –
thought up such a thought as that!
I, old matchmaker, devised
a fine match: with a mouthless oak!
Couldn't I see he was a fool,
oaken oaf, deaf as a stump?
Not smell the carrion? My flair,
my brains, my eyes, where were they all?
For the smoothness of his chin,
for the blondness of his curls,
for the pinkness of his mouth,
this old woman got it wrong.
Ah but, though the pleasure failed,
still the honour can be saved.

Woman-loather, dog, look out!
No one witnessed what you did!
What's unseen's not done, at night
any thief is in the right.
Woman-strangler, dog, look out!
To Theseus's eyes
by her body I'll swear

that black is white,
by her turf I'll swear
that white is black,
true will appear
false; false, true,
thus I'll present it.
And never again
shall red lips or brown
eyes . . .

ONE OF THE MAIDS
      The king comes!

NURSE
    . . . hang upon trees!

MAIDS *(one after the other)*
    – He's crossing the moat!
    – He's entering the courtyard!
    – Who'll hold the stirrup?
    – Who'll greet our dread king?
    – There's no-one. – A desert.
    – Who'll open . . . – Who'll welcome . . . ?
    – Who can? – Who will tell him?

NURSE
    I will, hunched
from telling stories,
I'll swear by her fame
that left is right,
I'll swear by her tree
that right . . .

THESEUS *(entering)*
        Am I sane?
No sounds, no smoke.
House, courtyard – dead.
Is the foe in the house?
Is a god in the house?
Has the plague attacked?
Has my son – died?
What's happening here?

NURSE
Old king, it is fate.

(pointing)

Behold – the queen.
It wasn't the plague
but impudent looks.
Oh king! Not a spell
but impudent speech,
fatal quaking of walls,
an impudent rake!
Sire! Wherever she goes,
he's there, everywhere!
She sits down, he'll squeeze up,
stroke her shoulders, the thief.
Wherever she looks,
there he is! Night and day:
'I'm kin, am I not?'
Sleep – he's walking around,
drink – he's filtering his drinks,
eat – he's there, putting bread
in his mouth, down his throat.
She felt death in her bones,
stopped eating. – Behold . . .
But the poor girl found
no peace in her bed.
A branch in the forest
kept knocking, calling.
Upon that branch,
that girdle, she bade
farewell to our world.
King – most holy –
my weaving, his cleaving,
or reaving . . .
. . . . So queenly!
See, her good fame
was dearer than daylight
(the branch was close by).
See, her honour
was dearer than life

or smoke of her hearth . . .

THESEUS
His name!

NURSE
                    Ah king!
It cannot be uttered!
The sound would bring down
the palace, set fire to
the forest, fill clouds
with thunder, Phaedra's
flesh would rise up . . .
He's no invader!
He treads his *own* floor!
You eat, sleep, together!
Your breath, your light,
your glory. As though
a right-hand finger
were nameless, alien –

THESEUS
My son?

NURSE
            Your own son.

THESEUS
What, he?

NURSE
            Yes, he.

THESEUS
Where is he – my son –
was my son, now a dog –
we wait – see *her* there,
the work of his hands –
but he – where is he?

NURSE
That ostler? Gone
to be nurse to a wolf?
Bravo! Now gone

after others, your own
dispatched and disposed of!

THESEUS

Father Poseidon!
Elder and Ocean!
See this old man,
blackened like turf,
sad as a raven
– Theseus once! –
do you recognise
the young lion on the Square?

Would I know him myself?
Shaggy-browed Prince,
roll back your waves
thirty years and hark
through the roar of time:
'Call and I'll help!' –
So the god's pledge
to the valiant youth.

Father Poseidon!
Elder, far-seeing!
Best of all wives . . .
my hearth – defiled . . .
honour – defiled . . .
he did worse than kill!
Oh less than an hour
have I loathed my son!

Prince of great quiet,
Prince of dread voice!
Commander of chasms,
rivers and seas!
Supporter of strength!
Of Theseus's once!
Under his feet
make the ground quake!

Thwart him, a clod
in his path, pack of hounds
at the coward's heels!
The thief turns aside
but the wave's there before him:
ahead – great gulfs,
at his back – dread heights.
Fast the thief but the wave shall fell him.

Let that driver's rib-cage burst!
Let him be bewitched and cursed!
Dogs, come tear him limb from limb!
Curse him! Curse him! Three times cursed!

CHORUS OF MAIDS *(speaking together)*
Who says you're dead? You're sleeping!
In fine array, anointed.
Who says you're hapless? Happy!
Foliage and flowers at your bedside
brought from the wilds and gardens,
and all the fresh young bushes
without their thorns and spines.
Not in grief you sleep, in glory you sleep.

When you wake you'll sweetly dip
your two feet in the rivulet.
For they plucked you like a flower
from above the one who hung.
Oh friends, we were mistaken! –
Not cursing but rejoicing
is needed, praise to the bough.
Not as whore you sleep, as wife you sleep.

Come and stand around the tree!
Come and honour Phaedra's bough.
Phaedra's story,
Phaedra's conscience,
Phaedra's girdle, Phaedra's bough.
Come celebrate a dreadful fruit!
Phaedra's shyness,

Phaedra's boldness,
Phaedra's deed and Phaedra's sweat.
Two things are immortal green:
laurel and myrtle, secret kin!
You as 'wife of Theseus',
he as 'Phaedra's husband' – both
shall abide triumphantly,
both supreme, in equal part –
sword of valour, bough of faith,
myrtle leaf and laurel leaf.

Come, let us bless the tree of love,
planted by your forefather!
You as 'wife of Theseus',
he as 'Phaedra's husband' – so
long as ever the world shall stand,
with morning time and evening time,
honour the little myrtle bough!
You sleep, no mortal but eternal.

Round and round the rescuing bough
let us, in Phaedra's memory,
dance a new dance,
let the dance
forever in her name be danced!
You fertile ones and idle ones!
Come to our goodly Troezen tree,
each of you, if only once,
leave your bed, as Phaedra did,
without a qualm, without a sound
abandoning her bed, her life . . .
Tears, be dance! Chorus – a choir
not of wailing but of praise!

Your twentieth spring or thirtieth,
whether wife or whether maid,
each and every one of you,
bring your offerings to the tree
and celebrate the victory
of woman's *brow* – and drain the cup!

Tears, be dance, and hail, be hail –
not of weeping but of leaping!

Seen from turrets,
seen from branches:
stepson blazes,
stepmother quenches.
Seen by horses,
seen by the ostler:
stepson groans,
stepmother chases.
– Passion's my right!
– Honour's my shield!
For stepmother – glory,
for stepson – laughter.
In royal halls there's
flattery and truth . . .
– Stepson builds,
stepmother smashes.
Battle, using
rouge for chalk.
Stepson tortures,
stepmother withers.
– Why not my right?
– Wanton, get out! –
Stepmother's glory,
stepson's shame.
'I've no more tears!
End, end my woes!'
Stepmother rises,
stepson follows.
And if no third,
no tree, divides them . . .
Stepmother hangs,
stepson walks by. . .
Womanly honour,
you're beyond all bounds!
Stepmother's glory,
stepson's . . .

MESSENGER

          Horrible
news I bring!
Sire, be brave!
By the will of the waves,
take in a new cypress
and dig a new mound.
Dead – your begotten!
Your life will be dust!
There came a great wave
with the face of a bull,
it galloped, outgalloped
the charioteer,
it poured like steam
at the rider's heels –
he turns to one side
but the wave is there! --
back – but the bull
already sends
his minions, ball after
ball of foam,
the horses panic,
they snort with fear.
The bull is as big
as a house, as high
as the sky – a mountain!
Ocean – no water,
bull – but no horns . . .
The horses . . . the reins . . .
the best of drivers –
reins torn from his grip,
eyes torn from their sockets,
spokes from their axles . . .
A bull? Or – what? . . .

THESEUS

Poseidon, saviour,
Prince!

MESSENGER

      A hero

gone.

THESEUS
I'm avenged.

CHORUS OF YOUNG MEN
Tell it or conceal it?
Real or a chimera?
Lying, no longer standing,
lying, no longer driving,
loins are all a-gallop,
every sinew gallops –
he who left by chariot
comes back on a litter,
travels like an old man.
Slumbering or drunken?
Just now he was flying,
now he's being carried.

Lightning! The two-wheeler!
Fine path – for the fearless!
Where's the whip he cracked,
wheels he flew on, axles,
carriage – where? The driver
spilt the cart! In splinters!
Sets out in a chariot,
comes back on a litter.
Pivot of the kingdom –
down to a hovel.
Unrestrainable –
now immobile.

Tenderly he cared for
you – far more than any
care of men for women!
Horses, horses, horses –
why did you use the driver's
nape to scour the coastline?
He who left by chariot
comes back on a litter.
Was the path too twisting?

Was he spurred by Bacchus?
Moments ago, a leader –
now they pull and drag him.

What makes sinews pulse and
kindles feet – you knew it!
Gods, ye gods, ye gods, oh
why is he, your favourite,
exiled from good earthly
rye to faceless regions?
Setting out by chariot,
home upon a litter.
Who with? No one! Some
would go with him, the striplings . . .
Now our own coeval
has become eternal.

Brow as clear as marble –
its like will never be seen.
O Artemis, O virgin
twin of Phoebus – is our
young Hippolytus's
fervour so requited?
Setting out by chariot,
coming back by litter . . .

THESEUS *(blocking the way to the body)*
Carriers, stop!
Chorus, be still!
That isn't my son!
Since when have we called
poisoners of wells,
venomous beasts,
reptiles – our sons?

CHORUS
Sire, since when
is a son a reptile?

THESEUS
Reptile's a word

too kind for him!
Away with the canine
carrion! Away
over the wall!
Better he'd *spilt*
blood of his kin!
Incest shall find
no shelter, no roof.

CHORUS
Shall we pass or enter
an impious shelter?
Thundering, not raining,
raging, not lamenting.
Shall we pass, or lay this
dust here? Heaven will murmur!
Gravel – not paternal
arms, the resting place for
sons. Reared by a lioness?
What – would the lion weep?
Not give due food of the dead:
poppy, nard, but poison . . .
– Oh how gently, gently
we have borne this sleeper! –
Not with laurels but shame
the king greets his son.
Is he then unworthy
of funereal fabrics?
He whose beauty moved the
very stones to mercy!
In a curl on his temple –
look – a wet honeysuckle
petal lies undamaged.
He – your fresh young stem,
your palace-wilding –
bloomed like honeysuckle
round his father's tree-trunk!

Have you *seen* a reptile
with features so frank and gentle?

Pebbles pitied him – and
yet his father's pitiless?
Look at him – take and warm him,
cheeks and limbs and shoulders.
Stones, we know, are kinder
than gods – who sooner trample
roses than soar in the heavens!
Kinder than gods – oh surely
not kinder than a father?

SERVANT *(entering)*

Pardon one who may bring distress.
Yet these scattered and broken bits,
put together, may form a *whole*,
useful for you to know, perhaps?

(Hands over the fragments)

This was no accident, nor fright:
something hurled in a fit of rage,
flung in anger with face convulsed.
Seeing how far apart the pieces
fell from each other, it must have been thrown
from very high up, from the very height
of honour, highest of fortresses.

(pointing to the body of Hippolytus)

He will say nothing, we'll hear from this
wax.
Read . . .
The sleepers know.

THESEUS

Headed 'secret'. .
Signed 'Phaedra'.
Letters – you burn!
Am I blind? Am I mad?
Headed . . . Signed . . .
And in between . . ?

Oh delusion! He's honest! Chaste!
What do I see? A eulogy

for Hippolytus in Phaedra's hand!
His virtue's triumph! His tablet of gold!
Horses, gods, my wife – oh why?
Grief, grief! This wreath of honour
to virtue – *she* is condemned by it!
Hammer, don't fall; reaper, don't reap!
My son's glory – my wife's disgrace!
Snow and resin, pitch and salt –
my loved one's snow, my dear one's pitch –
how low she is beside his height!
Stabbed through the heart! A tablet? Wax?
My breast split open – cut in half!
A loved one's honour, a dear one's shame.
Black is she by his purity!
Such delusion! My son! My wife!
How black she is . . . Oh, what did the gods
mean by mixing honey and pitch
together in a single scoop?
My dear son cold in Phaedra's lecherous
sweat . . Fingers of Aphrodite's
hatred! Oh my son, forgive
an old man! Wilds of Aphrodite's
hatred.

(to Phaedra)

This . . . you . . .
the whole of you not worth Hippolytus's
little finger!

NURSE

Sire, she's chaste!
Bull and bough,
corpse and corpse –
work of these hands,
work of these lips.
This. These.
This one's. This.
To all your kin
I am the grave.

'Handsome, tanned,
bowing, tall . . .'
I seduced!
I convinced!
Mine the plan!
'Do you have sons?
The bold one's right!'
I alone.
'Youth is sweet!
Youth is soft.'
See, old man,
Phaedra's sin.
Phaedra's vice.
Phaedra's? No!
She – the braid:
I – the braider.

In – your – ear.
It's – my – trade.
What? Phaedra?
No – the *pimp*!
Want him? Catch
the nightingale?
Phaedra – wax.
Mine the hands.

Nothing at all but her aged husband
did her beauty desire or hope for.
Nothing at all of crimes, sly doings
did her innocence know or even guess at:
whether a knock from left or right . . .
a bed gone cold, a husband old,
widower's customs, fatherly habits –
would have been all, would have mouldered away . . .
No glance at any scarlet carnation
would her beauty ever have given,
she'd have eyed no more than an earthen basin . . .
and all would have passed and vanished away,
but for my itching and urging and murmuring,
but for my drone of devices and secrecies.

What's to be done with baldness, decrepitude?
Our hair thins out and nobody wants us,
even the mangy ones no longer look at us!
Teeth drop out – food's still on the plate:
lips, lips, lips – oh the sweetness of loving!
Teeth drop out – does that stop the saliva?
Empty maw, unforgettable memory!
At least have a chew with another's teeth!
Empty maw, unforgettable memory!
At least press a breast with another's breasts!

'*My* time's gone!
You – enjoy!'
Nothing more sad.
Old man, punish!
My time's gone!
Flog, but know
in this place
I am the gods.

THESEUS

Madwoman, enough!

NURSE

Not to tree-stump, not to bee . . .
I'll whiten you with my own blackness.
Sleep, my sweet one.
Waft, my myrtle!
By my fabling
I'm blacker than soot.
Whiter than glory
you have remained.
Whip me, sire, I'll bask in it!

THESEUS

Witch, what for? Bawd, what for?
What – over agonies? Over the dead?
Come to your senses, stupid old woman!

In the world there are mountains and valleys,
in the world there are high ranks and low ranks,

in the world there are plagues and landslides,
in the world there are gods and goddesses.

Hippolytus' horses and Phaedra's bough aren't
old woman's intrigues, they're ancient knockings
of fate. Can human beings shift mountains?
They equip us. You – the equipment.
Hippolytus' foam and Phaedra's sweat –
not old-woman tricks – but an old accounting,
a long-known, very ancient quarrel.
No one's to blame. All are blameless.
Don't sear your eyes, don't tear your hair:
the name of Phaedra's fatal love – a
poor woman's love for a *poo*r young child – is
Aphrodite's hatred of me, the
garden destroyed on the isle of Naxos.
In different form, and in different fashion,
still the same guilt is being punished.
New lightning, old thundercloud.

Where the myrtle rustles, full of her groaning,
raise up for them a double grave-mound.
There at least (pity and peace to both)
may Hippolytus's bone be bound to Phaedra's.

LONG POEMS

LONG POEMS

New Year's Letter

Happy New Year – new world – new land – new roof!
Very first letter to you in your new
– *not* lush (for ruminants): that's a misunderstanding –
place resounding, place of loud redounding,
like Aeolus's hollow tower. First letter
ever sent to you from yesterday's
homeland (where without you I'll be drained and
wretched), now just one among the myriad
stars . . . Retreats, departures have their logic:
'dear-beloved' becomes just anybody,
charm 'unheard-of' – is no longer heard of.
Shall I tell you how I heard that you had . . . ?
No earthquake, not a crashing hurricane.
Someone entered, no one special (none can
ever be as loved as you) – 'How grievous . . .
in the *Daily* and the *News* . . . You'll give us
something on it?' 'Where?' 'The mountains.' (Window
framed in pine-trees. Linen.) 'Don't read the papers?
So you'll . . . ?' 'No.' 'Oh, come on.' 'Let me off, please. . .
too hard.' To myself: *I don't sell Jesus.*
'In a sanatorium.' (Rented heaven.)
'When?' 'Mm, yesterday, it seems, or even
day before . . . Shall you be at the Alcazár?' 'I can't – my family . .' *Just not Judas.*

*

Happy (born tomorrow!) year's-beginning . . . !
Shall I tell you what I did on learning . . . ?
Shsh . . . I almost said it. Force of habit.
Ages, now, ago, I started wrapping
life and death in quotes, like obvious gossip.
I did nothing. Someone seemed to be there,
doing something, but it made no shadow,
had no echo!

Tell me about your journey:
how your heart went tearing – not to pieces –
forward. Like a ride on Orlov horses,
quite as swift, *you said*, as actual eagles,
taking your breath away . . . Or still more powerful?
More delightful? Anyone who's flown on
genuine Russian eagles can't be thrown by
heights, descents. We're blood-bound to the other
world: whoever stayed a while in Russia
saw *that* world in *this*. So transit's easy!
Life and death I mention with a secret
smile of irony – your own will meet it!
Life and death I mention with a footnote,
asterisked (the night I'm hoping for: a
hemi-globe not cerebral but stellar,
full of stars!) –
            And please, dear friend, remember:
why my German writing has surrendered
to Russian isn't what they often say: that
dead men (beggars) see no difference, they'll eat
all you give them, never bat an eyelid!
No, the reason's that the *other* world, our
own world (this I realised, aged thirteen, when
visiting the monastery), isn't
languageless, it has all languages.

*

So I'm asking, not without dejection:
are you still asking how we say, in Russian,
Nest? We've got one rhyme for 'nests' (or *gnyòzda*),
one that covers all nests: 'stars' (or *zvyòzdy).*

Have I become distracted? But distraction
of my mind from you just cannot happen.
Every word, *Du Lieber*, every project
leads to you, no matter what the subject.
(Germanic's more germane to me than Russian,
yet Angelic's most!) There's no location
where you are not. Or no, there's one: the coffin.
Is everything the way it was, or wasn't?

(Don't you, just a little . . . no? of me, there?)
Rainer – with the same surroundings, feelings?
Tell me definitely – I am insisting:
First view of the universe, first vision
– naturally, the vision of a poet
in it – and your last view of the planet,
given you once, you only, in entirety!
Not of poet plus dust, spirit plus body
(take them separately – they're both offended),
but of you-plus-you, by you cemented –
(being Zeus-born doesn't mean you're best), your
Pollux-self united with your Castor,
you as grass-and-herb with you as marble.
Not a meeting, not a parting – eyeball
confrontation: very first of partings,
first of meetings . . .
                    Tell me about looking
down at your hand (all marked with inky traces)
out of so many miles away – how many? –
out of such endless height with no beginning,
far above the crystal Mediterranean
surface and those numerous other saucers.
All as it wasn't, and, for me too, all as,
past the last suburban edge, it will be.
All as it never was, and is already.
– What's a little extra week to one who's
finally signed off! Where *else* to turn, to
gaze, with elbows on the velvet rim, than
out of this to that, and out of thát one
back to this one with its many sufferings?
Here I live: Bellevue. A minor borough
built of nests and twigs. Exchanging glances
with the guidebook: Bellevue – prison with splendid
view of Paris – palace of the Gaulish
gargoyle – Paris and some nearby places . . .
Leaning an elbow on the scarlet parapet,
how absurd our Belvederes and Bellevues
'may' (we guess) – or *must* (to give my own view) –
seem to you up there in heights immensurate.

All those deviations. Details. Hurryings.
New Year's at the door. Who shall I clink with
over the table, and to what? And drinking
what? Here's cottonwool for beer-foam. Chiming
clocks. What for? And what have *I* to do here?
What can *I* do in the New Year's uproar
with my inner rhyme going: 'Rainer/dying'.
For if such an eye as yours has darkened,
this means life's not life and death's not death, it
means – I'm guessing, when we meet I'll grasp it –
neither life nor death exists, but something
new, some third thing. So then, to that new thing
(spreading straw for twenty-seven – what Heaven
for nineteen twenty-six to end with you
since it began with you as well!) – shall I now
over a table unsurveyable,
touch my glass's glass to yours with tender
clinking? Oh, not in the beer-house manner.
I-thou merge in silent rhyme, the third thing.

I can see your cross across the table.
So many places out of town, and so much
room! And why does a bush wave? It must be
waving to us! These places – all for us and
no one else! Pine-needles! Foliage! Places
solely for you and me – for you and you. (No
need to say, to be with you I'd even
join a mass meeting). Months! Not only places!
Weeks! And rainy suburbs, all quite free of
people! Mornings! Everything together
not even started on by nightingales!

*

True, I can't see well, I'm in a crater;
true, from high up, you can see much better.
Nothing ever came of our relation.
So completely, purely, simply nothing,
so appropriate to our own dimensions
that there isn't anything to mention.
Nothing except – but don't expect the extraordinary

(anyone out of order's in the wrong) but –
something somehow entering – what kind of
new order of things?
                         The eternal chant goes:
nothing! If only something, by some feature,
hinted at something distantly, if only
shadow of a shadow! Never mind if
just 'that day', 'that moment', just 'that house':
even a convict, sentenced, dragging fetters,
still gets gifts from memory: 'that mouth!'
Or were we simply being too scrupulous?
Out of all *that,* only the other *world* was
(only the other light was) ours, as we are
only a light-reflection of ourselves –
so in exchange for all this, all *that other . . .* !

*

Happy new least-built-up of all environs –
new place, Rainer, new world, new light, Rainer!
Happy extremest promontory of the proven –
new eye, Rainer, and new hearing, Rainer!

*

Things all hindered you.
Even passion, friends.
Happy new sound, echo!
Happy new echo, sound!

*

Often I wondered, sitting on the school-bench,
what are mountains like in Heaven, and rivers?
Are the landscapes nice without the tourists?
Am I right, Rainer, that Heaven is mountainous,
thunderous? Not the sort for widow-claimants.
Must be more than one Heaven? Maybe terraced?
One above the other? Heaven can*not* be
(judging by the Tatras) *not* an amphi-
theatre (with the curtain down on someone . . .)
Rainer, am I right that God's a *growing*
baobab? Not Louis, not *roi soleil.* There

must be more than one God there? And, higher
up, another?
                    And what's writing like, then,
in your new place? Anyhow, where *you* are,
poetry is! You yourself are poetry!
So how is writing in that pleasant life
lacking desk for elbows, lacking brow for
cupped palm . . . ?
                    A note, please – usual cipher!
Rainer, are you enjoying the new rhyming?
For, to explicate the word correctly:
'rhyme' – what else – conceivably – can – Death be
but a row of new rhymes?
                    Language-learning's
finished. Now a whole new set of meanings
and consonances. There's nowhere else to
go to.
        Au revoir. Till our reunion!
Shall we meet? At least we'll sing in unison!
Happy new earth, Rainer, unknown to me –
all of myself to you, and all the sea!

                    *

Send word – we mustn't pass each other by.
Happy new sounds, new tracing of them, Rainer!

                    *

Carry the sacred gifts up a ladder of sky.
Happy new laying on of hands, then, Rainer!

                    *

Held in my palm so nothing drops upon it.
Over the Rhone, over the Rarogne,
over the endless, obvious separation.
Into the hands of Rainer – Maria – Rilke.

Poem of the Air

So here is a couplet
to start with. The first nail.
The door had gone silent
like one with a guest who waits
outside it. He stood like
a pine-wreath (ask widows why),
all full of composure
like someone the master's call
has followed, a guest who
is watched-for. Let's say all filled
with patience like one with
the hostess's signal – sign
of darkness! – that lightning above
the servants! Alive or
a ghost – a guest who has heard
a knocking, unstopping,
past bearing – we die from this –
of the hostess's heartbeat,
a birch-tree beneath the axe.
(Prised open, Pandora's
casket, that box of cares!)
In-comers are numerous,
but who is it waits, not knocks?
Quite sure of a hearing
and timeliness. Leaning, he
is sure of an answering
ear (it's your sureness of me).
Not doubting an entrance.
The sweet (when we only play
at fear) special manner
of lingering – with key in hand.
Despising emotions
and high above husbands, wives –

that monastery, Optina,
gave up its very chimes.
A soul with no layer
of feelings. And fellah-bare.
Door – tense with alertness.
Can't that be said too of ears?
They stood up like horns of
a faun or like 'Squadron: fire!'
A tiny bit more and –
the door would become unhinged
by force of the presence
outside it. Thus sinews quake
in hours of great passion,
being stretched beyond limit.
Yet no knocking came. Floor – floated.
Door – flew to the hand.
The darkness – a jot – retreated.

II

Absolute – this naturalness.
Stillness. Sense of right.
Ordinary staircases,
normal hour (of night).
Flat along the wall a spread
shape of one who's breathed
scent of gardens, patently
letting me step ahead.
Into night's full godliness,
into the sky's full
height. (Like rustling larches, like
foam edging a bridge . . .)
Into total mystery
of the hour and place.
Total invisibility
even in the shade.
More than black as pitch – by far
blackest-pitchiest!
(Carmine, red of cinnabar,
staining our irises.

Now my retina has sieved
'world' to *this* and *your,*
beauty shall not tarnish my
eyeball any more.)
Dream? But that's at best a word.
What's beneath, inside?
Seemings? Let me try to hear:
We – yet a single stride!
Not the paired, harmonious
double-orphan step,
but a lonely – everyone's –
step while still enfleshed.
Mine. (It isn't holes that shame,
but the urge to patch!)
Something should be levelled out:
either you – descend
one inch, to that sovereignty
all the thinkers own!
Or – and I'm already heard:
I no longer sound.

III

Absolute and perfect rhyme.
Rhythm – my own at last!
Just as once Columbus did,
I greet an earth unknown:
air. Forget pedestrian
truths! A ground with great
strength of rebound – womanly
bosom underneath
trudged and worn-down soldier-boots.
(Mother-breast beneath
baby-feet . . .)
                    A step
into tautness. Which negates
any thought that this
path is easy. Taking on
sphere-resistance means
hiking through Russian rye, antique

rice – China, through you! –
like a shouldering throng against
the sea – for 'against' read
'with zest' – I fight like Hercules!
Emanation of the earth.
The first air is dense.

You my dream? Or maybe I'm
yours? Nonsense! A theme
fit for profs. I'll go by feel:
we – yet a single sigh!
Not a joined and unitary
twin-asthmatic sigh,
but the sigh of solitary
confinement: is it high
yet, the Dnepr? That Jewish sob,
zithering: is God deaf?
Something should be put to rights:
either you a breath's
length give in, to every head
living – (this I dread)
or – and I'm already freed:
I no longer breathe.

IV

Time of siege in Moscow when
typhoid fever struck!
Over now. All suffering done,
down the stony sack –
down the lung! Investigate
mucus! Air's gate –
opened up. The Pale
of Settlement – torn down.

V

Mother! – as you hoped, the air's
fighter lives! But why
give him apparatus? He's

himself entirely sky!
Firmament, be spread below
the fragile flying boat . . .
yet he's lung-light through and through –
why the loop, the dead
noose? A splash and rinse and flow . . .
Why pity him?
Don't be sorry for the pilot!
This – *is* his flight!
Don't attire his bits of bone
in shroud and grave-stone.
Death's a course on how to float
in air – it's nothing new.
(Ludicrous to make a search . . .
for what? Propellers, screws?)
All you air-Achilleses,
all, and even *you*:
don't breathe fame, the atmosphere
breathed by those below.
Death's a course in how to float:
everything shall start
over again . . .

VI

Glory to thee who let gaps be wide open:
I'm no longer weighing.
Glory to thee who let roof-tops be broken:
no longer hearing.
Solar-initiate, I'm no longer peering.
Spirit: not breathing.
Body that's solid is body that's dead:
conquered the downpull.

VII

Lighter, no skiff lighter
lying on seashore mica.
O how light the air is:
rare and ever rarer . . .

Slide of ludic fishes –
tail-of-trout elusive . . .
O the air is streamy!
streamier than speeding
hound through oats – and slippery!
Soft as hair– as wafty! –
of just-crawling infants –
watering-cans aren't streamier!
More: it's streamier, even,
than a lime-bark lining
freshly stripped, or onion.
Through pagoda-music
born of beads and bamboo –
through pagoda-veilings . . .
splashing! move for ever . . .
Why is Hermes winged when
fins would be more (floating)
fitting? Look, a downpour!
Rainbow-Iris! Shall we
move through your shower of Cashmere,
Shemakhán . . .
                                An upward
dance. . . Paths from hospitals:
first the dust can't pull you,
then can't grip your footfalls.
Fathomless, yet firm as
ice! The law of all
absences: earth's surface
first won't hold you, then de-
-weights you. Nymph? Or naiad?
Peasantwoman-gardener!
Age-old loss of body
when it enters water.
(Water-turbulation's
splash. A sandy slide.)
Liberation from the earth.
The third air is void.

VIII

Greige, the greyness streaking
Granddad's sweepnet, striping
Grandma's plait. But sparely!
Sparse, more sparse than droughted
millet. (Shaven, naked,
spikes of it all grain-shed.)
Oh how sharp the air is,
sharp, more sharp than jagged
combs for raking dog-locks.
Happy space of coppiced
woods. In starts of waking
(nodding off, *we*'d call it!),
crisscrossings' delirious
scantness, links all vanished.
Oh how sharp the air is,
sharp, sharper than scissors,
or – than chisels. Lances
into pain – it's waning.
Sparsely, as when fingers
fence the heart, or (straining)
teeth withhold our reasoning
from the lips' shy credo.
Oh the air is riddling:
creativity's sieves are
not more filtering (silt is
wet, but dry – infinity).
Filterier than Goethe's
eye or Rilke's hearing . . .
(God but whispers, fearing
his own powerfulness.) It's
only not more filtery,
surely, than the hour of
Judgment . . .
         Ache of backbone,
reaping – why give birth, then?
Tread the whole no-harvest,
tread the whole no-yield of
height . . . Tread the furrows

where no ox, no plough . . .
Excommunication from the earth.
The fifth air is sound.

IX

Thundering lungs of pigeons –
they are here-begotten!
Oh the air is humming,
humming even more than
New Year tunes! Or axe-drone
hewing into oak-roots.
How the air is humming,
humming even more than
recent grief, than monarchs'
thank-yous . . . more than sonorous
hail on tin, more droning
than the roll of stone, or
trove in national folk-song,
great-mouthed, unforgotten.
Surging warbler-gullets –
thunder here-begotten!
Moving through the lachrymal
cupreous droning, like a
singing breast, of John the
Snowstorm-theologian?
Palate of Heaven's vault, or
lap of the tortoise-shell lyre?
Humming more than the Don's
hum of war, and stronger
than the scaffolds' mowing . . .
Moving over curvings
more severe than mountains:
curves of sound, like glebes in
Thebes the no-man-founded.
Seven – the layers and ripples!
Seven – *heilige Sieben*!
Seven, ground of the lyre,
seven, ground of all being.

Since the lyre's foundation is
seven, the world's foundation is
lyric. Thus the Theban
glebes glide to a lyre . . .
Oh, though still in the body's
kiln, 'lighter than feathers!'
Age-old loss of body
through the ear. Whoever
turns to ear will turn sheer
spirit. Leave to time
the letters. Are we moving
in pure sound or pure
hearing? Dream's pre-tuning.
Ecstasy's pre-fever.
Humming, more than mainsail
in equinoctial headwind.
More than crack of cranium
epileptic, famine
ventral. Only not more
humming than the paschal
sepulchre . . .

X

      Hum beyond humming:
through lulls of power, intermittences,
mobiler even than motion these
lulls and pauses and breathing-gaps –
grain-locomotives that pause to gasp . . .
Alternation of all the best
beckonings as from deities:
air alternates with better-than-air!
And – I won't call them sensuous –
lulls: transferrals, like changing trains,
leaving the slow for the interspace –
lulls, little halts along the ways,
halts of the heart when the lung gives off
'Okh!' in half-stoppages of breath –
lulls in a fish's sufferings,

lulls – interrupting, cutting off
current, or vapour abruptly thinned,
lulls and hiatuses, sundering
pulse – but this isn't clear enough:
'lulls' are a lie when there are *spasms*
of breath . . . Chasm unfathomable
of lung surprised by eternity.
Not all say that.
Some call it 'death'.
Separation from the earth.
Air is finished. Firmament.

XI

Music rending like a rack!
Breath, always in vain!
Over. All the suffering's done,
down the gaseous sack
of the air. Now, compass-free
up into heights! Child,
like and into father. Hour
when heredity
really tells. A firmament!
Road for unbraked heads!
How to sever: fully torn
sinciput from shed
shoulders. Ground of groundless beings!
Hermes, we are yours!
Here's the full and accurate
feeling of a head
borne on wings. There aren't two ways:
only one – and straight.
Sucked up into space, the spire
drops its church – to time.
Not in a day but gradually:
God, through the obscure
wilds of feelings. Into heights
like a bow-shot! Not
into a realm of souls, but full
dominion of the brow.

Limit? Grasp: when Gothic church
catches up with its own
spire, and – having calculated
all things, number-hosts! –
in that hour when Gothic spire
catches up with its own
meaning . . .

Attempt at a Room

I

Stick-in-mud walls were counted up
long before. But – a quirk? fortuity?
Three walls I have memorised.
Fourth – I can't give a guarantee.

Who can tell, with their back to the wall?
May be there, but it may be *not*

there. And wasn't. A draught blew. But
if not wall at one's back, then what? Whatever you *don't* like. Telegram:
'Tsar – abdicates. – Dno.' A message

needn't come letter-post. Urgent wires
every moment and every place.

Used you to play the piano? Draught
blows, moves like a sail. Your hands go
woolly. Up flies the music score.
(Don't forget that the ninth is yours.)

That never-ever-seen wall – I know
what its name is: wall of the back

seated at keyboard. Better, at
writing-table, or even at
shaving. (This wall's trick is: change
into a corridor down the mirror.

Carried you over – you took a glance.
Chair metaphoric, of emptiness.)

Chair for all who cannot get in
by door – the threshold senses footsoles!
That very wall out of which appeared –
you (I'm hurrying through the past) is

there between us, still an entire
paragraph. Dánzas-like you'll rise

up from behind it. For *that* same wall –
chosen, invited, with weight and time (I
know its name: it's – wall of the spine) –
enters the room as Danzas, not as

D'Anthès. Turn of the head. We start?
This is you at the end of ten

stanzas. Lines. An attack by eye
on rear. But leave this behind-back category:
ceiling undeniably – *was*.
Not insisting 'as in a parlour',

maybe even a bit on the slant.
(Bayonet-thrust on the rear – of powers) –

Now the clench of the cerebellum.
Like a clod of earth the back
sank. It's that solid wall, Cheká,
wall of dawns – that is, dawn-lit shootings,

much preciser than shady gestures –
into the back from behind the back.

Shooting: *that's* what I can't take in.
But leave this behind-wall category.
Ceiling – undeniably there –
finished. (Why we want it will come

later.) I'll return to the fourth
wall, the one from which, stepping back,
cowards stumble. – 'Well, was there a floor?
Surely we need something underneath our . . ?'
Yes. Not everyone does, though. Up
trees, swings, horseback, tightrope, orgy. . .

up and up!
        In the *other world*
we've all got to plant our gravity-laden
heels in vacancy.
                Floor – for feet.
How embedded is man! How fettered!
Ceiling – so there will be no drips –
(ancient torture by drops – remember,

one per hour?). So no grass gets in,
floor so earth won't invade the house –

brought by those whom even a stake
won't deter on Walpurgis Night!
Three walls, plus a ceiling and floor.
That enough? Then make your appearance!

II

Will he rattle a shutter, give
warning? Hurriedly organised,
whitish on grey, this room is no
more than a sketch in a pocket-book.

Never a roofer or plasterer –
dream. A custodian in wire-lessness.
Deep in the gulfs under eyelids some
'he' has discovered a 'she' in there.

Never deliverer or furnisher –
dream, more naked than shallows at
Rével. The floor not gleaming. This –
really a room? Just flat surfaces.

Landing-stages are friendlier!
Something out of geometry:
chasms in some little calendar,
well understood, though belatedly.

And is a desk just a phaeton-brake?
Desks require to be elbow-fed.
Elbow all over an incline – then
Even that will have desk-likeness.

Just as babies are stork-conveyed,
things will arrive when they're needed. No
fretting a mile in advance. You'll see
chair and guest simultaneously.

III

All will appear,
don't build or fix.
Under the sign
of – shall I say which?

Forest-depth
of mutualness.
That hotel –
'The Souls' Tryst'.

IV

Meeting-house. All others –
parting-houses, even if
south-by-south. Is it hands that
serve here? No, something more

quiet than hands, lighter, cleaner.
Renovated junk plus
services? Starving, gaunt
penury is left out there!

Yes, here we're touch-me-nots, and
quite rightly. Slaves of hands,
hands' – thoughts, hands'– conclusions,
tips, ends, the ends of hands . . .

No fervid cries 'where are you?'
I – wait. Gestures take
over all the serving, silent,
in the palace of the mind.

V

Only the wind is dear to a poet!
Corridors are what I'm sure of.

Passing through is base, for armies.
Must keep going and going, so that

suddenly, middle of room, resembling
the god with the lyre . . .
                           – the path of poetry!

Wind, wind, above our forehead,
raised like a banner by our striding!

Now the hackneyed old words 'and so on' –
corridors: distances made homely.

Distance silent and fast with rook-like
profile of unbeliever, made

childfoot-size, in a rainy raincoat:
rhymes so dear to me: waffle, trifle,

duffel . . . somewhere in peacock mantle
there's a tower and its name is Eiffel.

As to a child a river's a pebble,
and any bit of distance is little,

so in a child-mind, stringed and steeped,
distance is just a governess holding

holdalls, too modish to tell us *what's*
being dragged along over there in carts . . .

Space – reduced to a box of pencils . . .
corridors: the canals of houses.

Fates and festivals, deeds and deadlines –
corridors: flowing streams in houses.

Five a.m. with an unsigned letter:
down the corridor go not only

brooms. Smells of peat and caraway.
Occupation? Corridor-worker.

Only asking for what was milled
in corridors by the Carmagnole!

VI

Who built (or dug) the corridors
knew how to curve them, so
blood would have plenty of time to
turn at the heart's acute-

angled corner, that magnet
attracting thunders! Time
for the heart's island to be
awash from every side.

This corridor is created
by me – don't ask me why!
So the brain should have plenty of
time to inform the entire

line – from the 'No Embarking'
sign right up to the heart's
junction: 'It's coming! Shut your
eyes if you're going to jump!

Else – off the rails!' This corridor's
made by me. Not a poet:
artless. The brain to have plenty of
time to allocate seats.

A meeting's a place, after all, a
list, calculation, sketch, of
words that don't always fit, and
gestures, invariably wrong.

So that love is in order,
all of it. So you'll like
all of me, every crease of
lips or dress! Of brow.

VII

They all knew how to fix their dresses!
Corridors: the tunnels of houses.

Like an old man led by his daughter –
corridors: the ravines of houses.

Friend! As in that dream or letter,
it's *me* like a shaft of light upon you!

You're falling asleep, your eyelids closing,
and here am *I*, like a premonition:

light. At the last possible moment,
I – a single eye of light.

VIII

Well and then?
Dream – in tune.
There was – lifting,
ballroom bowing

of brow – and brow.
Your – brow
ahead. Uncouth
rhyme: mouth.

IX

Was it because the walls were gone –
undeniably the ceiling leaned

down, and only the vocative case
flowered in mouths. Floor – undeniable

gap. Through the gap, green as the Nile,
ceiling undeniably floated.

As for floor, what else can one say
to floor but 'Be damned!' Whoever cares
about dirt on floors? No chalk? – Look up!
The whole poet – by a single dash –

holds on . . .
                Over two bodies' *nothing*
the ceiling undeniably sang –

with all the angels.

NOTES AND SYNOPSES
FURTHER READING

Notes and Synopses

Notes to *Phaedra*

Tsvetaeva divided her drama into four 'pictures' (*kartiny*). I have called them 'scenes' because 'pictures' or 'tableaux' suggest something static. There is indeed a pictorial quality to each scene: a picture of huntsmen in a forest; of a queen lying ill on her couch, talking to her companion; of a young prince first with his servant and then with the wild-haired queen; finally, of the queen hanged in a tree among mourners. But every 'picture' also contains a good deal of action. I have made some slight alterations to Tsvetaeva's stage directions. – A.L.

Scene One

Page 33: *Callisto*
Nymph in the train of Artemis.

Page 36: *dawn-god's / twin*
According to the myth, Artemis was twin of Apollo.

Page 38: *fence of stems*
Artemis (Roman 'Diana') was so angry when seen by Actaeon bathing naked in a stream that she changed him into a stag and his hounds tore him to pieces.

Scene Two

Page 48: *pigeon milk*
Something non-existent or foolish.

Page 50: *You're her sister twice*
Both Phaedra and Ariadne were daughters of Minos and Pasiphaë and the Nurse considers their having married the same man a kind of second sister-hood – see Introduction, 'Related narratives . . .'

Page 55: *what she did to him*
This may refer to Antiope's intrusion upon his wedding feast – see Introduction, 'Related narratives . . .'

Page 63: *splash of / cowardly oars*
After leaving Ariadne, Theseus rowed away over the sea.

Page 64: *sacrificial slabs*
On which Hippolytus made sacrifices to Artemis.

Page 65: *My name means 'shining'*
phaidrós is Greek for 'bright, shining'. Note also line 14 of Phaedra's last long speech to Hippolytus in scene three: '*Shining*? . . .'

Scene Three

Page 70: *honeycombs*
The Troezen area of Greece was famous for its honey industry.

Page 73: *Goddess of Foam*
Aphrodite (Roman 'Venus') was born from the foam of the sea.

Scene Four

Page 85: *young lion*
Theseus, as a youth, was often praised for his lion-like courage.

Page 87: *woman's brow*
Tsvetaeva uses brow (*lob*) to signify intelligence or greatness of mind; see the very end of 'Poem of the Air': 'full / dominion of the brow'.

Page 92: *nard*
Or spikenard – an aromatic balsam used by the ancients to make a valuable ointment.

Synopsis and notes to 'New Year's Letter'

The Russian title is the single adjective 'New Year's'; its neuter singular ending could suggest 'letter'.

Except for four trimetric lines near the end, this poem is written entirely in trochaic pentameter, an unusual line-length for Tsvetaeva.

Synopsis

The poet sends a New Year greeting to Rilke, who has just died. He is now in a new place full of sound, from which the earth seems just another star. She tells how a friend informed her of his death –

and asks Rilke about his journey to the other world, for him a swift and easy journey because, having been in Russia, he has seen the 'other world' in advance.

She explains that she writes in Russian, not German, since the other world is multi-tongued; and recalls Rilke asking her about Russian words.

All topics lead to him. What is it like to have died, how does the cosmos look, how does the earth look from up there, how does it feel to have all aspects of oneself united?

She imagines him looking back to earth, and herself looking across to him, as if at the stage from a box at the theatre. How absurd earth's suburban places must seem to him now!

How can she join in any New Year clinking of glasses when Rilke has died, and how can there be such a thing as death in application to him? Instead of touching glasses, she touches him in rhyme across the table of infinity, thereby creating something new, a 'third' thing.

All the rural places where they might have met! In reality there were no meetings at all, so no memories remain of their relationship, whereas other people, even convicts, remember things seen and shared. All she and he had together was their possession of the other world.

Again a greeting, and now more urgently the question: what is Heaven like – surely not static but ever growing, changing, with numerous levels . . . ?

. . . and poetry-writing in that new place? She begs for a message.
Finally she places the poem, like a letter, in Rilke's hands.

Notes

Page 101: *world*
'world' (*svet*) could alternatively be rendered as 'light', and 'land' (*kray*) as 'edge'.

Page 101: *Aeolus*
God of the winds; the author re-imagines his walled-in island as a tower.

Page 101: *Someone entered*
In fact it was her friend, the literary critic Mark Slonim.

Page 101: *Alcazár*
A restaurant in Paris.

Page 102: *Orlov*
A Russian breeder of fast horses, his name deriving from *oryol*, 'eagle'.

Page 102: *German writing*
Tsvetaeva spoke German fluently and had been writing to Rilke in German.

Page 102: *monastery*
In the graveyard of the New Virgin Monastery in Moscow (in the original its name is given) Tsvetaeva's beloved cousin Nadya was buried, along with many famous persons.

Page 102: *Nest*
This is also the German for 'nest'; in his last letter, Rilke wished he could remember the Russian for it.

Page 103: *Pollux . . . Castor*
Twins born of Leda and Zeus. Pollux, who alone of the two was immortal, divided his immortality with Castor.

Page 103: *Bellevue*
The Paris suburb where Tsvetaeva lived. *Belvedere*, too, means 'beautiful view'.

Page 104: *nineteen twenty-six*
The whole exchange of letters between Tsvetaeva and Rilke took place in 1926.

Page 105: *other* world . . . *other light*
I have made two lines out of one, to accommodate the two meanings of *svet* (see note to page 101, line 1).

Page 105: *Tatras*
Mountain range between Czech lands and Poland.

Page 105: *baobab*
An enormously thick-trunked tree found in Africa and India.

Page 106: *Rhone*
Near where Rilke spent the last years of his life. He was buried in *Rarogne*.

Synopsis and notes to 'Poem of the Air' (see also Appendix 2)

I have divided this poem into eleven numbered parts in accordance with the breaks.

My translation reflects Tsvetaeva's metrical patterns wherever possible (rhyme is included much more randomly). In the original, Part I alternates lines of two amphibrachs with the same plus a single stress [x / x x / x — x / x x / x /]; Parts II, III, IV and V mainly alternate two trochees plus one dactyl with two trochees plus a single stress [/ x / x / x x — / x / x /] ; Part VI alternates lines of three dactyls and a trochee with lines of one dactyl and a trochee [/ x x / x x / x x / x — / x x / x]; Parts VII, VIII and IX are in trochaic trimeters [/x / x / x]; Part X is in variable lines of, mainly, dactyl-trochee-dactyl [/ x x / x / x x] ; and Part XI alternates lines of two trochees plus dactyl with lines of two trochees plus single stress [/ x / x / x x — / x / x /].

Synopsis

An upward journey is made, through seven levels of air, to a place beyond breathing.

I — A passionately desired guest is waiting silently outside a closed door. Like a hostess, the one inside has sent him a sign of welcome. Ordinary emotions do not belong in this scene of mounting desire for a union between this-world and other-world. Somehow the door opens and . . .

II — it feels absolutely right to be outside in the dark with the shadowy guest. Now colours, too, and ordinary pleasures of perception are renounced. Though at first she begs her spectral companion to descend a little so as to accompany her, she herself rises to be level with him, and her footsteps become silent.

III — Again this change feels right, like perfect rhyme or rhythm. Air is difficult to move in, but she is glad of its challenge. This 'first air' is thick, or dense.* Again she asks her invisible guide to yield a little, this time by slightly breathing; again he does not and she, instead, gives up breathing.

IV — Untrammelled climbing in air is like the removal of quarantine from Moscow when a typhus epidemic is over, and like the breakdown of the Jewish Pale of Settlement.

V — Addressing the mother of a pilot, she asks why, being air himself, he needs apparatus in order to fly. Death is a course in flying.

VI — Praise for the one who made holes in the world for us to go up through.

VII — The air now attained is wonderfully light, rare, slippery, watery and, like water, reductive of weight. She ascends not like some fabulous naiad, but truly physically, like a peasant woman who slides into a pool. This leads up to the 'third air' which is empty* . . .

VIII — and sparse and sharp, full of well-placed gaps like a sieve, thus resembling great creative minds, which filter out all that is irrelevant. Only the Last Judgment would sift things more finely. Speculation on the futility of human labour: we should renounce earthly things altogether.

IX — The 'fifth air' is sheer sound* and is like birdsong, birds' heartbeats, forest felling, kingly speeches, hail-falls, folk-music, the Book of Revelation, an ancient lyre, scaffolds (swish of the axe?), mountains (the wind there?), and the building of the city of Thebes; the mystical number seven is celebrated. The sound of the level now reached is like that of sailing at the equinox or a cracking head before an epileptic fit. Only Christ's tomb is more resonant.

X — Now the air is largely 'better-than-air' – it is all lulls, gaps and pauses; but 'not-air' still alternates with air. Finally giving up breathing, she attains what others might call 'death': the end of air.

XI — Breathing and its products, such as music, are over; she is free to speed upward, unhindered. Winged heads have shed their bodies, spires have shed their churches, the 'brow' predominates; there will yet be a moment when the 'spire / catches up with its own / meaning'; the poem ends with a row of dots.

Notes

I

Page 107: *guest*
Generally taken to represent Rilke; disappears from the poem after Part III.

Page 108: *Optina*
Optina Pustyn' – a well-known monastery.

II

Page 109: *lonely – everyone's*
In life, our footstep has the sound of only one person's, betraying our existential loneliness.

---

* In 'thick', 'empty', 'sound' (*gust, pust, zvuk*), the shared vowel resembles *oo* in English 'loose'.

Page 109: *It isn't holes that shame . . .*
Holes, in shoes or clothes, are not shameful; shameful is the obligation we feel to patch them: there is no shame before nature but only in society.

III

Page 110: *Dnepr . . .*
Russian for the River Dnieper. Is the river swollen, the ice about to break, release from prison imminent?

Page 110: *Jewish sob*
Perhaps of David the Psalmist, wanting God to hear his playing.

V

Page 110: *the air's / fighter*
At the end of the manuscript of 'Poem of the Air', Tsvetaeva noted: 'Meudon. In the days of Lindbergh'. On May 21 and 22, 1927, Charles Augustus Lindbergh became the first person to cross the Atlantic in a solo, uninterrupted flight.

Page 111: *lung-light*
Russian for 'lung' (*lyogkoye*) also means 'light' (adjective). I have used both meanings.

Page 111: *loop*
The Russian phrase for 'to loop the loop' uses words meaning 'dead noose'.

VII

Page 112: *Hermes*
Greek god of (among other things) trade, messages and travel.

Page 112: *Iris*
Greek goddess of the rainbow.

Page 112: *Shemakhán*
This calls to mind the beautiful maiden in Pushkin's 'Tale of the Golden Cockerel' who appears to Tsar Dadon at the peak of his conquest, seduces and ruins him.

VIII

Page 113: *greige*
Greyness, cf. French *grège*.

Page 113: *nodding off*
What others call waking up, poets call falling asleep, because sleep is full of insights.

IX

Page 114: *John . . .*
Mark 3:17 – 'James the Son of Zebedee, and John the brother of James [he surnamed] Boanerges, which is, the sons of thunder'. Tsvetaeva renames John

'the Snowstorm-theologian', replacing thunder with snow and suggesting, with 'theologian', the author of the Book of Revelation.

Page 114: *lyre*
The first seven-stringed lyre was made, by Hermes, from the shell of a tortoise.

Page 114: *the Don's / hum of war*
This may recall the battle of Kulikovo on the upper Don in 1380 (first important victory over the Mongols who occupied Russia for two centuries) and, more probably, recalls battles between Red and White armies in the Civil War which followed the October 1917 Revolution.

Page 115: *the Theban / glebes glide to a lyre*
The ancient city of Thebes was partly built by Amphion and Zethus, sons of Zeus, Amphion's stones moving gently into place in response to the sound of his lyre.

X

Page 115: *grain-locomotives*
Trains on which speculators from the towns travelled into the countryside at great risk to their lives to exchange urban objects for flour during the time of War Communism (1918–21).

XI

Page 116: *like and into father*
Ditya v ottsa means 'the child takes after (is like) the father', but the context suggests also the literal meaning of these words: 'child *into* father' (a movement upward into God).

Page 116: *brow*
Thought, or mind, goes beyond flesh *and* spirit.

Synopsis and notes to 'Attempt at a Room'

I have divided the poem into nine numbered parts, according to the changes of metre.

The metrical figures vary with each part, but almost all are based on trochee (/ x) and dactyl (/ x x). Part I has / x / x x / x / alternating with / x / x x / x x /x ; Part II mainly /x x / x /x x ; Part III is the only instance of iambics: x / x x alternating with x / x / ; Part IV has / / x / x /x alternating with / / x / x / ; Part V / x / x x / x / x ; Part VI / x / x / x alternating with / x x / x / ; Part VII / x / x x / x / x ; Part VIII / x / ; Part IX / x / x x / x /.

Synopsis

This is a difficult poem, often opaque and often dream-like. Its chief preoccupation is the 'attempt at (constructing) a room'. It is also concerned with writing:

references to table (or desk), to paragraphs and to 'stanzas, lines' point to the act of writing and to the text in process. The repeated words 'leave this category' are the poet's instructions to herself about what to write next. Yet there are very few signs to show how any one idea or image links to another. Never saying 'this resembles . . .' or 'suddenly I remember . . .', the poet abruptly brings in a remembered or resembled idea, leaving the reader to contrive the connection. The following summary contains a number of my own contrivings.

I — The poem starts in mid-imagining of the room. Three walls are easy to think up, but the fourth one (behind you) is not. (Another poet will be invited to the room, for a meeting of two poet-minds.)

The invited poet used to play the piano; piano-playing in the poem-room will be disrupted by wind blowing in through the unwalled space. The pianist's back is like a wall (being the vertical area nearest to the observing eye?), but the desired fourth wall is reflected in a mirror (a shaving mirror?) in which, given the infinite depth of mirrors, it becomes a corridor.

Violent deaths – Pushkin's duel, murders by the Cheka – somehow get into the poem. Pushkin perhaps enters through the invitation to a present-day great poet; this leads to the notion that the desired wall (friendly to poets, because they will be able to meet when it is in place) resembles Danzas – Pushkin's friend, his second at the fatal duel, and of course the antithesis of D'Anthès, who killed him. The Cheka enters the poem through, first, perhaps, the thought of the pianist's unprotected back (as a back connotes shooting or a bayonet-thrust), and, second, its actual killing of poets.

Leaving the motif of violent deaths, the poet resumes construction of the room – its ceiling and again its fourth wall. Cowards would protest that they couldn't get in even if the fourth wall were there, since there was no floor. But – not everyone needs a floor! Some people, instead of being inert or moving for ever downward, can climb and fly up – into the 'other world'! The poet grieves that most people are obsessed with their houses instead of with upward flight.

The guest should arrive, now that all but the fourth wall is ready.

II — Waiting for him, she looks at the room that has begun to be made, and sees: pallor, bleakness, sketchiness, flatness, and the way it is obviously only a dream: 'This – / really a room?' But seems to regain optimism by considering the solidity of the writing-desk: presses elbows into desk and again expects the guest.

III — 'Room' becomes 'hotel': in their actual correspondence in 1927, Pasternak told Tsvetaeva that he dreamed he rushed downstairs in a hotel to find her waiting for him like a vast cloud of radiance.

IV — 'Hotel' continues through references to servants and 'services'. She and he seem to be together there now. But bodilessly, as 'touch-me-nots', gesturing without hands. It is a 'palace of the mind'. (Is this failure or the hoped-for meeting?)

V — Celebration of wind, speed and corridors. ('Wind, wind . . .' may recall the wind of revolution in Blok's 1918 poem 'The Twelve'). Praise of an army, because its very 'base' (its form of stillness) is movement, a passing through, never stopping. If you keep moving you will come to poetry.

Another view of corridors: they make distance homely; and this brings in childhood, through the way distance, in childhood, was presented as not frightening but comforting, 'childfoot-size'; a child could rhyme the distant Eiffel Tower with familiar words. Similarly, instead of contemplating a whole river, a child is fascinated by just one of its pebbles, thinks of distance merely as the place the governess arrives from, and knows nothing of political horrors. Corridors are, moreover, places where revolution is prepared: an early-morning servant may hasten through them to deliver anonymous letters.

VI — (Do corridors become analogous to channels and arteries of the human body?) 'This' corridor, 'created by me', is perhaps the poet's own body. It seems also to resemble a railway on which a suicide is imminent; excitement and danger bring back the expectation of a meeting – which cannot be perfect, but she does hope she will be entirely liked. (In the course of the poem there are many references to parts of the body, not especially female or erotic: back, hands, footsoles, head, cerebellum, heels, feet, elbow, forehead, blood, heart, brain, lips, brow, eyelids, mouth, and, finally, bodies . . .)

VII and VIII — She sees the loved poet asleep, with herself looking at him like a point of light; they will meet in a dream.

IX — Collapse of the room. Walls are gone, ceiling leans down, floor is a hole. Nothing is left even of language except a bit of punctuation – a dash, onto which the poet holds.

But – floors are despised anyway, and the ceiling, the highest part of the room, is not quite gone, only leaning over, and – singing! (Upward aspiration wins out over house-building?)

The room does not get built, but the poem of the room does get written.

Notes

I

Page 118: *Stick-in-mud walls*
The Russian is *Steny kosnosti* (walls of inertia), i.e. walls of houses whose inhabitants are content with the everyday.

Page 118: *Dno*
The name (meaning 'Bottom') of the town, near Pskov, at whose railway station (it is generally believed) on the night of March 14, 1918 Tsar Nicholas II signed the announcement of his abdication from the Russian throne.

Page 118: *the ninth is yours*
This seems a private message from Tsvetaeva to Pasternak, suggesting either: 'it's your ninth year' (he played the piano from childhood on, as did she), or:

'the ninth wave (i.e. disaster) awaits you', recalling the beginning of her 1923 poem 'Ariadne': 'To be left behind is to be etched / In the chest – the blue tattoo of sailors! / To be left behind is to be displayed / To the seven seas . . . Doesn't it mean, to be / the ninth wave, which shall sweep [you] off the deck?'(The poem is addressed to Pasternak, who went back to Russia in 1923, giving up the chance of meeting her. In the legend, Ariadne was left by Theseus on the Isle of Naxos.)

Page 119: *Dánzas*
Pushkin's friend, who acted as his second at his duel.

Page 119: *D'Anthès*
Pushkin's adversary in the duel.

Page 119: *Cheká*
The secret police force set up by Lenin in December 1917.

Page 120: *Walpurgis Night*
A Spring festival in many countries of Europe, with wine, dance and bonfires.

II

Page 120: *Rével*
The old name of Tallinn (Revala).

III

Page 121: *That hotel*
In his dream (see synopsis) Pasternak saw Tsvetaeva as a cloud of radiance at a hotel door.

IV

Page 122: *palace of the mind*
Or, literally, 'of the psyche', 'psyche' being Greek for mind, soul, spirit, breath.

V

Page 122: *the god with the lyre*
Apollo, god of poetry and music.

Page 122: *waffle, trifle, / duffel*
These replace the Russian words *grifel'*, *tufel'*, *kafel'* (slate-pencil, slipper, stove-tile).

Page 123: *the Carmagnole*
A song, 1792, popular in the French Revolution after the fall of the monarchy.

VII

Page 124: *in that dream*
Probably again a reference to Pasternak's hotel dream.

Further Reading

Tsvetaeva's work in English translation[*]

(i) Poetry

Selected Poems, translated by Elaine Feinstein, London, 1971, reprinted 1981

After Russia, translated by Michael Naydan with Slava Yastremski, Ann Arbor, 1992 [bilingual edition containing numerous poems written in 1923, the year Tsvetaeva began thinking of writing a drama based on the Phaedra story. Among them are two poems in which Phaedra (as then conceived) speaks to Hippolytus (see pages 154–55 of the present book for a translation of one of these), as well as another poem relevant to *Phaedra*, 'Ophelia in Defence of the Queen', and the ten poems addressed to Pasternak in the 1923 poem-cycle 'Wires']

Poem of the End: Selected Narrative and Lyrical Poetry, translated by Nina Kossman with Andrew Newcomb, Dana Point, CA, 1998 [bilingual edition]

The Ratcatcher: A Lyrical Satire, translated by Angela Livingstone, London, 1999; Evanston, IL, 2000

Milestones, translated by Robin Kemball, Evanston, IL, 2003 [bilingual edition of the poems published in 1922 as *Versty*]

(ii) Prose

A Captive Spirit: Selected Prose, translated by Janet Marin King, Ann Arbor, MI, 1980, reprinted 1983 and 1994 [nineteen autobiographical pieces and one of literary criticism]

Boris Pasternak, Marina Tsvetaeva, Rainer Maria Rilke, *Letters 1926,* edited by Yevgeny Pasternak, Yelena Pasternak and Konstantin Azadovsky and translated by Walter Arndt and Margaret Wettlin, London, 1986; reprinted New York, 2001 [this printing contains an English translation, by Jamey Gambrell, of 'Your Death', Tsvetaeva's 1927 essay addressing Rilke after his death, pp. 321–50] [*Letters 1926*]

Art in the Light of Conscience: Eight Essays on Poetry, translated by Angela Livingstone, Bristol, 1992; Cambridge, MA, 1994; reprinted Tarset, Northumberland, 2010 [the title essay, 'Art in the Light of Conscience', is indirectly relevant to *Phaedra*] [ALC]

About Tsvetaeva

(i) Biographical

Simon Karlinsky, *Marina Tsvetaeva, The Woman, her World and her Poetry,* Cambridge, UK, 1985 [Karlinsky]

Viktoria Schweitzer, *Tsvetaeva,* translated by Robert Chandler and H.T. Willetts, edited and annotated by Angela Livingstone, with quotations from Tsvetaeva's poetry translated by Peter Norman, London, 1992

Lily Feiler, *Marina Tsvetaeva, The Double Beat of Heaven and Hell,* Durham and London, 1994

---

[*]According to which transliteration system is used, 'Tsvetaeva' can also be spelt 'Tsvetayeva' or 'Cvetaeva'.

(ii) Other

Joseph Brodsky, *Less Than One*, Harmondsworth, 1986 [the two essays on Tsvetaeva in this volume, namely 'A Poet and Prose' (pp. 176–94) which is about Tsvetaeva as a prose-writer, and 'Footnote to a Poem' (pp. 195–268) which analyses the long poem 'New Year's Letter', are widely considered to be the best studies of Tsvetaeva's style and thought] [Brodsky]

Barbara Heldt, *Terrible Perfection, Women and Russian Literature*, Indiana, 1987 [includes discussion of Tsvetaeva specifically as a woman writer, pp. 130–43]

Jane Taubman, *A Life Through Poetry: Marina Tsvetaeva's Lyric Diary*, Columbus, OH, 1988

Michael Makin, *Marina Tsvetaeva: Poetics of Appropriation*, Oxford, 1993 [her work is considered in the light of its use of literary forerunners and traditions] [Makin]

Olga Peters Hasty, *Tsvetaeva's Orphic Journeys in the Worlds of the Word*, Evanston, IL, 1996 [a study of the mythic in Tsvetaeva's work, with a detailed account of 'New Year's Letter' and a translation of it]

Tsvetan Todorov, *Marina Tsvetaeva, Vivre dans le feu. Confessions*, Paris, 2005 [parts of Tsvetaeva's diaries and letters, translated into French with commentaries] [Todorov]

Catherine Ciepiela, *The Same Solitude. Boris Pasternak and Marina Tsvetaeva*, New York, 2006 [a detailed examination, through their letters and poems, of the two poets' epistolary love-relationship, as well as of their relation to their changing times]

R.D.B. Thomson, 'Tsvetaeva's Play "Fedra": an Interpretation', *Slavonic and East European Review*, LXVII/3, July 1989 (pp. 337–62)

Alexandra Smith, 'Surpassing Acmeism? The Lost Key to Cvetaeva's "Poem of the Air" '. *Russian Literature*, XLV, 1999 (pp. 209–21)

The Phaedra legend and other *Phaedra*s

Robert Graves, *The Greek Myths*, Harmondsworth, 1955/1986

The Oxford Classical Dictionary, edited by Simon Hornblower and Antony Spawforth, Oxford and New York, 1996

Euripides's drama 'Hippolytus' (428 BC) has attracted many translators. The version by David Grene (in Euripides, *Four Tragedies*, vol. I of *The Complete Greek Tragedies*, translated by David Grene and Richmond Lattimore, Chicago, 1955) remains valuable. Among more recent translations are those by John Davie (in *Alcestis and Other Plays*, London, 1996), by Michael R. Halleran (in *Four Plays*, Newburyport, MA, 2004, which has full and useful footnotes), and a version by Anne Carson (in *Grief Lessons: Four Plays*, New York, 2006)

Seneca's 'Hippolytus OR Phaedra' (c. AD 50; the work is commonly referred to by either title) is translated by F.J. Miller in *Seneca's Tragedies*, London and Cambridge, MA, 1917/1960; and by R. Scott Smith in the Penguin Classics edition *Phaedra and other plays*, Harmondsworth, 2011)

Ovid's *Metamorphoses* (AD 8; prose translation by Mary M. Innes, Harmondsworth, 1955/1984; verse translation by A.D. Melville, Oxford, 1987) has three pages devoted to the death of Hippolytus with a brief mention of Phaedra (pp. 347–49 and 366–68 respectively), while Ovid's *Heroides* (verse translation of 'Epistulae Heroidum' by Harold C. Cannon, London, 1972) includes a long piece of verse imagined as a letter from Phaedra to Hippolytus

Racine's drama *Phèdre* (1677) is still available in the excellent Larousse single-text edition, Paris, 1933. Among the several English translations are the one by John Cairncross in the Penguin Classics edition (*Iphigenia. Phaedra. Athaliah*, Harmondsworth, 1963/1975) and the version by Ted Hughes (*Phèdre*, London, 1998)

Swinburne's 'Phaedra' (1864) is contained in *Poems and Ballads and Atalanta in Calydon*, Harmondsworth, 2000

Among twentieth-century dramas based on the Phaedra legend, the most notable are the following: Hilda Doolittle, *Hippolytus Temporizes. A Play in Three Acts*, Boston and New York, 1927; Robinson Jeffers, 'The Cretan Woman' in *Hungerfield and Other Poems*, New York, 1954; Tony Harrison, 'Phaedra Britannica (after Jean Racine)', in *Plays 2*, London, 1975/76). Eugene O'Neill's 'Desire Under the Elms', 1924 (in *Nine Plays*, New York, 1921–52) does not explicitly refer to the Phaedra legend but is often cited as based upon it

APPENDICES

APPENDIX 1

Translating *Phaedra*

Almost every line in this play has been hard to translate. Not only because of Tsvetaeva's neologisms, her archaic and folkish forms, her inventive ease with rhyming and her syntactical expertise, but because, even where the language seems simple, this is superb poetry, as hard to do justice to as any work of genius. Throughout, I have tried to bring the Russian meanings across into clear English as well as to reflect the rhythms which to the poet were so important.

Some individual words were particularly problematic. Two examples are *gádina* – the word of revilement with which Hippolytus rejects Phaedra, and *navazhdéniye* – Hippolytus's exclamation on realising Phaedra is his stepmother, as well as Theseus's on learning of Phaedra's guilt.

Gadina I at first wanted to translate as 'snake', but did not because a snake may be wise; 'vermin' would not do, being a collective noun; 'disgusting [or vile] creature' was too lengthy. After much pondering I settled on 'reptile', despite its feeling less violent than *gadina*.

For *navazhdeniye* I tried 'entrancement', but found it too pleasant for this context; 'hallucination' was too suggestive of illness, 'evil enchantment' too long, 'bedevilment' too colloquial. 'Delusion' I rejected as too plain, lacking any hint of the magical, but then, finding 'illusion' even plainer, I returned, *faute de mieux*, to 'delusion'.

One of the great pleasures of translating *Phaedra* has been precisely these concentrated searches for English equivalents to individual Russian words, searches which did, after all, often lead to satisfactory solutions. There was great satisfaction, too, in reflecting many of Tsvetaeva's metrical innovations. Sometimes these could be exactly rendered in English, but even where, more usually, they could not, I have found similar rhythms and have kept the shapes of her lines (see Introduction under 'Rhythms').

There is a further huge challenge to the translator of Tsvetaeva's *Phaedra* – her frequent introduction of elaborate and meaningful word-patterning. As an example I will take the speech in scene three in which Phaedra confesses her love to Hippolytus.

From Scene Three: Phaedra tells Hippolytus how she fell in love

1. Russian original:

... Началом
Взгляд был. На путях без спуска
Шаг был. Ошибаюсь: куст был
Миртовый – как школьник в буквах
Путаюсь! – началом звук был
Рога, перешедший – чащ звук –
В чаш звук! Но меднозвучащих
Что – звук перед тем, с незримых
Уст! Куст был. Хруст был. Раздвинув
Куст, – как пьяница беспутный
Путаюсь! – началом стук был
Сердца, *до* куста, *до* рога,
До всего – стук, точно бога
Встретила, стук, точно глыбу ...
– Сдвинула! – началом ты был,
В звуке рога, в звуке меди,
В шуме леса ...

2. Transliteration:

Nachálom
Vzglyád byl. Ná putyákh bez spúska
Shág byl. Oshibáyus'. **Kúst** byl
Mírtovyy – kak shkól'nik v búkvakh
Pútayus'! – nachálom **zvúk** byl
Róga, pereshédshiy – cháshch **zvuk** –
V chásh **zvuk**! – Nó mednozvucháshchikh
Úst! **Kust** býl. **Khrust** býl. Razdvínuv
Kúst, – kak p'yánitsa bespútnyy
Pútayus'! – nachálom **stúk** byl
Sérdtsa, *dó* kustá, *do* róga,
Dó vsegó– **stuk**, tóchno bóga
Vstrétila, **stuk**, tóchno glýbu ...
– Sdvínula! – nachálom tý byl,
V **zvúk**e róga, v **zvúk**e médi,
V **shúm**e lésa ...

[Metrical stress accented.
Underlined: words with vowel *u* stressed
or quasi-stressed.
Bold type: words here discussed.]

3. Word-for-word translation:

The beginning
a-glance was. On paths without way-down
a-footstep was. I'm-mistaken. A-bush was,
of-myrtle. Like a-schoolboy in letters
I'm-getting-lost! – the-beginning a-sound was
of-a-horn, turning – thickets' sound –
into goblets' sound! But brass-sounding-
  things,
what-is [their]-sound next-to that from
  unseen
lips! A-bush was. A-crunch was. Moving-apart
the-bush, – like a-drunkard dissolute
I'm-getting-lost! – the-beginning a-knocking
  was
of-a-heart, *before* the-bush, *before* the-horn,
before everything – a-knocking, as-if-a-god
I-had-met, a-knocking, as-if a-lump-of-earth
– I-had-moved! ... The-beginning you were
in-the-sound of-the-horn, in-the-sound
  of-brass,
in-the-noise of-the-forest ...

[Hyphened words represent a single Russian
word. Russian has no 'the', 'a'; 'am', 'is', 'are' and
can omit personal pronouns.]

4. Final English version:

The beginning
was – a glance. A footstep. Paths with
no way down. I've got it wrong, there
was a bush, a myrtle bush. I've
lost my way, I'm like a schoolboy
muddling letters! – the beginning
was a horn's sound – sound of thickets –
turning into a sound of goblets!
But what's the sound of ringing brass
next to a sound that came from unseen
lips! A bush. A crunch. Pulling
the bush apart. I'm getting
lost, I'm like a sluttish drunkard.
In the beginning was a knocking
heart – *before* the bush, *before*
the horn, before it all – a knocking,
just as though I'd met a god – a
knocking, just as though I'd moved a
boulder! The beginning was
you, in sounds of horn and brass
and rustling forest ...

[Underlined: words with stressed *u*.]

What can, and what cannot, be translated here? The narrative *can* be, as can the speaker's intense excitement and confusion. The analogies can, on the whole, be translated; so can the fact that, after 'glance' and 'bush', references are not to things seen but to things heard, all of these being recapitulated at the end of the speech in the emphatic sounds of 'horn', 'brass' and 'forest'.

Among elements that cannot be translated are, first of all, the qualities peculiar to Russian, such as the flexibility of word-order and 'semantic aureoles' of case-endings, grammatical features Tsvetaeva makes characteristically strong use of. Secondly, there is rhyming, and hers is unusual (all but one of the rhymes in this passage being of penultimate vowels only). And there is her way of letting meanings arise from phonic resemblances, as when the sound 'of thickets', *chashch*, leads to the sound of goblets, *chash* (nor does it seem strange here that someone confused by sudden love can enjoy such a linguistic event). Yet what is supremely untranslatable is a subtle interweaving, throughout this passage, of certain significant monosyllables.

There are six of them, all sharing the same vowel (roughly the vowel in English 'doom'), and almost all sharing the same consonants: *zvuk* (sound), *kust* (bush), *stuk* (knock), *ust* (lips), *khrust* (crunch) and *shum* (noise). Each of the first three of these, after being introduced fully stressed (coinciding with an ictus in the trochaic verse) is later repeated, either once or twice, in non-ictus positions – that is, *as if not stressed*, although, as a meaningful monosyllable, it cannot be sped over: I am calling it 'quasi-stressed'. Thus *kust* reappears fully stressed one line later, while *stuk* (the knocking of the heart) merges into a twice-repeated and stressed *zvuk* at the very end of the speech, where both the rhythm and the word *shum* (noise, rustling) confirm two things. They confirm, first, that the speaker has after all managed to say the difficult thing she had to say, and, second, that a delicate musical development has reached its conclusion in a powerful final cadence. The masterly way in which this is done, and the way the other monosyllables, *ust* and *khrust*, along with several longer words which also have the stressed vowel *u*, variously contribute to the growing theme, might just imaginably find some brilliant equivalent in another language. But it could never be quite the same; the main poetic event here is embedded in the Russian language and eludes translation.

Monosyllables with the vowel *u* often play a prominent role in Tsvetaeva's writings, as they are linked for her with the importance, in her thinking, of *zvuk* (sound) and *slukh* (hearing), as well as with *ukho* (ear) and *dukh* (spirit); all this is discussed by R.D.B. Thomson in 'Tsvetae-va's Play "Fedra"' (see Further Reading). There are many examples of such words in the present volume, among them the heavily significant 'knock[ing]' (*stuk*) both in scene two (the lovesick Phaedra's heart) and in scene four (Theseus invoking the 'ancient knockings of fate'); throughout *Phaedra* there is the myrtle bush (*kust*) symbolising love, and, in 'New Year's Letter', the 'bush' that oddly waves to the poet, hinting at friendship, nature and home. In 'Poem of the Air' it is 'sound' (*zvuk*) that characterises the highest level of air before it becomes 'better-than-air', reminding us of the centrality of hearing and sound in Tsvetaeva's accounts of inspiration and poetic creation.

A.L.

APPENDIX 2

'Climbing the Air'

A respectful abbreviation of Marina Tsvetaeva's 'Poem of the Air'

I wrote the verses below immediately after completing the first draft of my translation of 'Poem of the Air' in 2002. They are meant neither as an alternative translation nor as an independent poem, but are offered as a possible help to the reading of Tsvetaeva's difficult poem; also as the sigh of relief they were to me upon my finishing that first draft. – A. L.

I

Who is that waiting
outside, silent?
(First nail hammered
in, by a couplet.)

Behind the alerted
door, like a pine-wreath,
the guest, certain
of welcome (my signal
flashes like lightning
over the shadows of
visitors, servants –
to him: 'Come in!')

My heart is pounding
like birch-trees falling –
axed, crashing;
like the evils flapping
their bird-wings out of
Pandora's casket.

He'll never come in
(though he's got the key!)

– he won't even knock.
He listens: I'm listening.
So is he a ghost?
But feelings aren't needed.

Unemotional
sinews yearn,
the floor – floats,
the door – leaps
into my hand, the
dark recedes.

II

And now it's becoming unutterably natural
to be out here in the dark with somebody
garden-surpassing, invisible, ghostly,
full of forbearance, walking behind me
under the high sky with its sound of
foam lapping at night-time bridges;
natural to give up longing for colours
for ever: my retina's finished its sifting
of this world (beauty) from your world, henceforth
the only desired one. We're two, yet a single
step is heard: mine. Oh, come down, be audible!
No. I go up, by an inch, to be soundless.

III

Perfection of rhyme and rhythm, Columbus'
view of a new earth: Air! – As bouncy
as woman's bosom to soldier or infant.
Taut and elastic this air, resistant –
I'm fighting through it, fearless from now on,
Herculean. The first air: thick.
But you – come down if only a breath's length,
please, give in to the living a little!
No. Instead I go up by an inch,
no longer breathing.

IV

Breathing was torment,
like typhus in Moscow,
the lung – a stone cauldron.
But air's gates have opened,
all its walls fallen.

V

Airmen don't need apparatus – the sky is their body!
Pilots don't need any aeroplanes – look, they're already
made up of lightness, height and the boundless!
Fame brings their grounding, alas! But in unfamed
flight they're Achillean, groundless.

VI

Now to give thanks – for the rifts in the stiff world
that let us escape it.
Thanks – to the holes in the roof where we hurl down
ballast. Unweighted...

VII

Light, rare, ludic, slippery, streamy
air like fleet elusive fishes,
air like speeding hounds through oat-fields,
not to be caught or held, it slides
like sliced onion, like lime-bark lining,
like bamboo curtains that veil pagodas
(Hermes ought to wear fins, not winglets),
showers all shimmery, paths releasing
dance – like entering water: weightless.
No more earth. The third air: empty.

VIII

Grey, grey, grey. A sweepnet
streaked with shapes, an aged hair-plait

striped with *greige*.
Spare, sparse, like spikes of millet
shaved by drought. Sharp as a comb's teeth
raking dog hair, spaced as coppiced
copses, scant as
linklessness when you're waking up
('falling asleep' is what I'd call it).
This air is sharper than scissors, chisels,
lances, scalpels – it's fiercer, sharper
than teeth clenched against chants of credos.
This air is a sieve, a filter, fine as
Goethe's eye or Rilke's hearing,
able to just-catch God's thin whisper.

Why have harvests? Choose the no-harvest!
Why have the ache of reaping? Why have
furrows, oxen, ploughing – give
all of it up! Prefer the no-ox,
no-plough, no-furrow.
Be done with earth.
The fifth air: sound.

IX

As axes drone,
so this air drones,
as monarchs drone
their fine monotones,
or as hail drones
on tin, or the folk
drone their poems,
or John the Divine
drones, intones ...
like sounds of scaffolds,
sounds of mountains,
glebes of Thebes
inspired by lyre-sounds...
Entering hearing
is like entering water:
absolute weight-loss.

The seventh air:
herald of rapture.

X

And now there are only the gaps, intermittences,
increase of space
between movements of power,
now there's the alternating and weaving
of something-better-than-air with air,
ecstatic stoppings of breath like a caught fish,
like cuts to electric current, hiatuses,
sunderings of pulse, and at last an end
to lung-work. Why do you call it 'death'?
It's separation, discovery.
It's firmament.

XI

An end to the pains
of music, of breathing.
Wing-borne heads,
ripped from futile
shoulders, dash
along, unbraked.
The Gothic spire
has dropped its church.
And – beyond?
That's the hour
when meaning's
over-
taken
by
. . .

APPENDIX 3

An earlier treatment of Phaedra: the poem 'Message'

This is one of two poems in the voice of Phaedra which Tsvetaeva wrote in March 1923, three years before she made a start on the drama, and which present a more demanding and forthright Phaedra. Here she calls herself, perhaps ironically, 'Mother' and, perhaps self-critically, 'your insatiable Phaedra'. The Phaedra of the drama does not give herself such names, and the poem should not be seen as adding to her characterisation, but instead as an interesting earlier conception of her.

Hippolytus: message from Mother – Phaedra – the Queen –
to you, a capricious boy whose loveliness runs
(like wax from sovereign Phoebus) away from – me.
So a message from Phaedra. A moaning of tender lips.

Oh soothe my soul! (Yet without the touching of lips
our soul can never be soothed!) To press upon lips
is to press upon Psyche, fluttering guest of lips . . .
Oh soothe my soul! – which means: oh soothe my lips.

I am weary, Hippolytus . . . Shame on the sibyls and whores!
This is no simple shamelessness crying to you! Only hands
and speech are simple. . . Beyond trembling lips and hands
there lies a great secret, with silence upon it, a sign.

Forgive me, virginal youth! And horseman! You hate
pleasure! – But this isn't lust! Nor the whim of a womb!
It's *she* who seduces! It's *Psyche*'s cajolery,
to hear how Hippolytus whispers, mouth to mouth.

'You should be ashamed!' Too late! It's the final surge!
My steeds have run wild! From the dizzy crest – to the depths –

I *too* am a rider! So from the heights of breasts,
the fateful twin hills, down to your breast's abyss!

(Or is it my own?!) Oh, be able! Be bolder! Be
gentler than if you were cutting marks in wax
(a dark heart's wax?) with a schoolboy's stylus . . . Oh let
Hippolytus' secret be read by the lips of your

insatiable Phaedra . . .

Translated by Angela Livingstone

Poetry in translation
in Angel Classics

GENNADY AYGI
Selected Poems 1954–94
Bilingual edition with translations by Peter France
978-0-946162-59-8

Gennady Aygi (1934–2006) is one of Russia's major modern poets, his free verse marking a radical new departure in Russian poetry. This is the most substantial presentation of his work published in the English-speaking world. 'Like Hopkins with English, Aygi makes the Russian language do things it has never done before.' – Edwin Morgan

PIERRE CORNEILLE
Horace
Translated by Alan Brownjohn
978-0-946162-57-4

This verse drama based on the legendary triple combat between two sets of brothers, the Horatii and the Curatii, to decide a war between Rome and Alba, lays bare the sinister nature of patriotism and has the power to challenge and disturb the modern reader with its unflinching reckoning of the personal cost of national glory. 'Corneille's rhyming alexandrines have been superbly translated into a flexible blank verse which captures the nuances of meaning.' – Maya Slater, *Times Literary Supplement*

HEINRICH HEINE
Deutschland: A Winter's Tale
Bilingual edition with translation by T. J. Reed
978-0-946162-58-1

This satirical travelogue on eve-of-1848 Germany is engagingly modern – on customs union, women, food . . . The wittiest work by Germany's wittiest poet. 'Reed succeeds beautifully in recreating the pointed, epigrammatic effect of the terse rhythm.' – Anita Bunyan, *Jewish Chronicle*

GEORG HEYM
Poems
Bilingual edition with translations by Antony Hasler
978-1-870352-97-0

The fullest selection of one of the major German modernist poets to appear in English. His apocalyptic contribution to the line of 'city' poetry from Baudelaire to T.S. Eliot abounds in explosive and shocking images contained in verse of strict classical form and metre. 'Hasler has achieved, not complete rhymes, but satisfying assonances, and has built his translations round them, preserving Heym's meaning with astonishing fidelity. His renderings serve as perfect examples of the art of translation.' – Ritchie Robertson, *Times Literary Supplement*

A Libris book distributed by Angel Classics

ALEXANDER PUSHKIN
The Gypsies
and other narrative poems
Translated by Antony Wood; wood engravings by Simon Brett
978-0-946162-72-7 (hardback)

Five of Pushkin's finest narrative poems: his first masterpiece *The Gypsies*, the ballad *The Bridegroom*, the comic tale of rural life *Count Nulin*, and the folk-tales The *Dead Princess and the Seven Champions* and *The Golden Cockerel*; with a substantial introduction, end-notes and an essay on problems of translation. 'Each of these five very different verse narratives has the tone and atmosphere of the original.' – Elaine Feinstein

RABINDRANATH TAGORE
Particles, Jottings, Sparks
Translated by William Radice
978-0-946162-66-6

The first complete translation of Tagore's 'Brief Poems' into English. These miniature fables, ironic quatrains, epigrams and fleeting verses jotted down throughout his life, originally published at widely spaced intervals in three separate volumes, are central to the poetry and spiritual personality of the great Bengali poet. 'Accessible ... insightful ... refreshing.' – David Moses, *Edinburgh Review*

Georg Trakl
Poems & Prose
Bilingual edition with translations by Alexander Stillmark
978-1-870352-71-0

The autumnal melancholy that predominates in Trakl's poetry heralds the calamity of the First World War. This is the most comprehensive edition of his work available to the English-language reader, who is enabled truly to get to grips with a central figure among the German Expressionist poets exhibiting what he once called 'the universal nervousness of our century'. 'Stillmark's selection is well designed, reflecting Trakl's wish for individual poems to be printed within larger cycles, and the translations themselves are accurate, unfailingly thoughtful and often very moving.' – Jeremy Adler, *London Review of Books*

A Libris book distributed by Angel Classics

Marina Tsvetaeva
The Ratcatcher: A lyrical satire
Translated by Angela Livingstone
978-0-946162-61-1

The first complete translation of Tsvetaeva's masterpiece, a satirical narrative poem on conformism and material prosperity, using the story of 'The Pied Piper of Hamlyn'. 'In a finely tuned line of verse in translation, the style of the original not only shines through the dense layers of a foreign linguistic element but seems to stand on a level with it, as if two brothers were comparing heights together . . . This was my experience when I read this translation.' – S. Nikolayev, *Literaturnaya gazeta*, Moscow